D1241901

# Maritime Issues in the Caribbean

# Maritime Issues in the Caribbean

*Edited by*
*Farrokh Jhabvala*

Proceedings of a conference held at
Florida International University
13 April 1981

*Florida International University*

University Presses of Florida
Miami

UNIVERSITY PRESSES OF FLORIDA is the central agency for scholarly publishing of the State of Florida's university system. Its offices are located at 15 NW 15th Street, Gainesville, FL 32603.

Works published by University Presses of Florida are evaluated and selected for publication, after being reviewed by referees both within and outside of the state's university system, by a faculty editorial committee of any one of Florida's nine public universities: Florida A&M University (Tallahassee), Florida Atlantic University (Boca Raton), Florida International University (Miami), Florida State University (Tallahassee), University of Central Florida (Orlando), University of Florida (Gainesville), University of North Florida (Jacksonville), University of South Florida (Tampa), University of West Florida (Pensacola).

Library of Congress Cataloging in Publication Data
Main entry under title:

Maritime issues in the Caribbean.

"A Florida International University book."

Includes index.
1. Economic zones (Maritime law)—Caribbean area—Congresses. 2. Fishery law and legislation—Caribbean area—Congresses. 3. Maritime law—Caribbean area—Congresses. I. Jhabvala, Farrokh.
JX4144.5.M37 1983 341.7'62'09729 82-20115
ISBN 0-8130-0753-4


Printed in the U.S.A. on acid-free paper.

# Contents

# Participants

Lewis M. Alexander, Director, Office of the Geographer, United States Department of State, and Professor of Geography, University of Rhode Island.

Lennox F. Ballah, Permanent Secretary, Ministry of External Affairs, and Head of the Foreign Service of Trinidad and Tobago.

Francisco V. García-Amador, Professor, School of Law, University of Miami.

Clarence P. Idyll, Senior Marine Analyst, National Advisory Committee on Oceans and Atmosphere, Washington, D.C.

Farrokh Jhabvala, Associate Professor, International Relations, Florida International University.

Julian S. Kenny, Professor and Head, Department of Zoology, University of the West Indies, Trinidad.

Vaughan A. Lewis, Director, Institute of Economic and Social Research, University of the West Indies, Jamaica.

Kaldone G. Nweihed, Professor, Social Sciences, Simón Bolívar University, and Director, International Research Program, Institute of Technology and Marine Sciences, Venezuela.

James A. Storer, Director, Office of Fisheries Affairs, United States Department of State.

Ronald W. Thompson, Director of Fisheries, Ministry of Agriculture, Fisheries, and Local Government, The Bahamas.

# Introduction

In early 1980 the Third United Nations Law of the Sea Conference (UNCLOS III) appeared to have reasonable prospects for an early and successful conclusion. The eight negotiating sessions that had been completed had produced an Informal Composite Negotiating Text (ICNT), upon which there appeared to be wide agreement. Differences between negotiating blocs and parties had been narrowed so that "aside from deep sea bed issues, the outstanding hard-core issues . . . no longer entail[ed] a general divergence of opinion on basic substantive questions."[1]

Progress toward the prevailing degree of agreement had been difficult and piecemeal.[2] Nonetheless, matters had arrived at a point where seasoned observers and participants shared the "general feeling that the conference was entering its final stages."[3] A year later, just before the conference's tenth session, there was the sense that barring unforeseen difficulties the loose ends of the draft Law of the Sea Treaty could be tied up during the next two sessions, thus setting the stage for the signing of the agreement by early 1982.

This assessment, however, clearly failed to recognize the importance and the extent of the change in government that had occurred in the United States with the elections of November 1980, and some days before the start of the conference's tenth session the Reagan administration imposed a pause upon the conference, precluding further movement toward the conclusion of the negotiations. A few weeks before the twelfth session (8 March –30 April 1982), the U.S. administration indicated its willingness to resume negotiations, insisting, however, upon a major revision of the proposed regime for seabed mining. Frantic efforts were undertaken to produce a compromise acceptable both to the United States and to the Group of 77. Despite some new concessions by the Group of 77, the United States refused to yield, and, when the draft treaty was put to a vote, the United States voted against its adoption.[4]

Paralleling the Law of the Sea (LOS) negotiations there have been numerous unilateral extensions and bilateral and other agreements between states establishing new coastal-state jurisdictions and sovereign claims in the oceans. According to one expert, who has also participated in the LOS negotiations, the provisions of the ICNT, and *mutatis mutandis* of subsequent versions of the draft text, "are rapidly being assimilated into national legislation and are increasingly relied upon as guides to state practice and *opinio juris*."[5] Regardless of the future treaty, therefore, new maritime norms deriving from, or at least contemporaneous with, the work of the LOS Conference are developing and becoming part of the body of international law.

Among the most important of these developments, particularly for Caribbean states, are the 200-mile exclusive economic zones and the fishing zones of similar dimensions that numerous states have proclaimed. In a semi-enclosed sea such as the Caribbean, extensive claims by "adjacent" and "opposite" states will inevitably overlap, necessitating delimitation agreements between the affected states. Further, as indicated by the refusal of some Caribbean states to make extensive maritime claims, the interests of some states, particularly fishing interests, are likely to be adversely affected by any Caribbean norm that establishes extensive maritime jurisdictions. Consequently, it may not be in the immediate interests of some Caribbean states to move toward the settlement of zone delimitation disputes, actual or potential. Clearly, these questions require consideration by interested persons and institutions.

With this view in mind, the Latin American and Caribbean Center at Florida International University decided in early 1980 that a conference to explore some of these issues would be worthwhile. With assistance from the Center for Latin American Studies at the University of Florida and from FIU's Student Government Association, The Conference on Maritime Issues in the Caribbean was held at Florida International University on 13 April 1981. The papers and comments collected in this book were presented at that conference. The Conference on Maritime Issues in the Caribbean comprised two sessions and a luncheon session. In the first session, on political and legal issues, Professor Vaughan Lewis examined the interests of the English-speaking Caribbean states in the LOS negotiations, juxtaposing these interests with the interests of continental American states such as Colombia, Venezuela, and the United States. Professor Kaldone Nweihed analyzed the question of delimitation of overlapping zones, developing possible guidelines for the numerous potential delimitations that may some day be undertaken in the Caribbean. Professor Francisco García-Amador commented on Lewis's paper, laying out grounds for a more optimistic outlook for the maintenance of the interests of the "zone-locked" and otherwise geographically disadvantaged states of the Caribbean region. Professor Lewis Alexander commented on Nweihed's paper, questioning some of his hypotheses and offering a different outlook on delimitation disputes in the Caribbean.

Mr. Lennox Ballah, in the luncheon address, examined the emerging Law of the Sea's overall impact upon, and consequences for, Caribbean states.

The second session focused on fishing interests. Dr. Clarence Idyll examined U.S. fishing interests in the Caribbean, and Professor Julian Kenny assessed the fishing interests of the insular Caribbean states. Mr. Ronald Thompson commented on Idyll's paper, agreeing with most of its aspects but dissenting from some, in particular the potential availability of hitherto untapped fish stocks. Mr. James Storer's comments included suggestions for possible institutional arrangements for the future development of Caribbean island fisheries.

The planning, organizing, and holding of such a conference draws upon the assistance and cooperation of many individuals, all of whom cannot be named here but to whom a debt is nonetheless owed. Special acknowledgments are due the Latin American and Caribbean Center at Florida International University, the Center for Latin American Studies at the University of Florida, and the Student Government Association at FIU, all of which contributed financially to make the event possible. Special thanks are due to Dr. Gregory B. Wolfe, president of Florida International University, who opened the conference and welcomed the participants; to Professors Mark B. Rosenberg, Anthony P. Maingot, Mark D. Szuchman, and Thomas A. Breslin, of Florida International University, and James B. Higman, executive director of the Gulf and Caribbean Fisheries Institute, for their valuable advice and support; to Ms. Carmen Figueredo, without whose energy and skills the organization of the conference would have been impossible; and to Kathy Feldman and Karen Pennington, who transcribed the conference proceedings and typed the manuscript of this book with much patience.

The three maps in Kaldone Nweihed's paper are reprinted from *Ocean Development and International Law* (1980), volume 1, number 1, by permission of Crane, Russak & Co., Inc. The map in Lennox Ballah's paper is from the Bureau of Public Affairs, Department of State, May 1982.

—Farrokh Jhabvala

## Notes

1. BERNARD H. OXMAN, *The Third United Nations Conference on the Law of the Sea: The Seventh Session (1978)*, 73 AM. J. INT'L L. 1 (1979) at 5.

2. *See*, for instance, SHABTAI ROSENNE, *Settlement of Fisheries Disputes in the Exclusive Economic Zone, id.* at 89.

3. OXMAN, *supra* note 1, at 3.

4. The vote was 130 to 4 (United States, Turkey, Israel, and Venezuela) with 17 abstentions.

5. OXMAN, *supra* note 1, at 38.

# The Interests of the Caribbean Countries and the Law of the Sea Negotiations

*Vaughan A. Lewis*

THE INTERESTS of the English-speaking Caribbean (CARICOM) countries in the United Nations Law of the Sea negotiations (which have occupied about the whole decade of the 1970s and which will, it is hoped, be concluded during the first half of the 1980s) are discussed here in the context of the interests and activities of the countries of the Caribbean archipelago as a whole and of those countries whose shores are washed by the Caribbean Sea.

The Anglophone countries that will be discussed include Guyana and the Bahamas, which, while not strictly within the limits of the Caribbean Sea, are part of the quasidiplomatic entity known as the Caribbean Community and have historical-political and cultural connections with the archipelago states.

There is some justification for devoting particular attention to the Anglophone countries within the context of what is sometimes called the Caribbean Basin. First, as newly sovereign states (among some still-dependent Anglophone countries), their historical experience of negotiations involving central questions of international law, and particularly sea law, is virtually nonexistent, although they have been the loci of complex negotiations undertaken by their metropolitan protectors. This distinguishes them from other states of the archipelago that achieved sovereignty in the late nineteenth and early twentieth centuries and certainly from the South and Central American states bordering the Caribbean whose participation in law and policy making is fairly extensive.[1]

Second, the discussions in the Law of the Sea Conference provide one of an increasing number of channels by which the newly (or soon to be) sovereign Anglophone countries are coming to terms, at diplomatic and other levels, with countries in the Caribbean Basin with whom they have hitherto had little formal contact. Such negotiations therefore induce consideration, or reconsideration, of the types and scope of Latin American and Caribbean relationships that are possible and beneficial for a set of countries whose diplomatic transactions have tended to be largely extrahemispheric (with the imperial power and its allies) or concentrated within CARICOM to which particular priority has been given.

It should be noted, of course, that in spite of restricted formal contacts, much movement of Anglophone peoples from the islands to the continental countries has taken place. Target countries have been Venezuela, Panama, Costa Rica, and Nicaragua, where work opportunities at various times have drawn individuals during the first half of the twentieth century.

The physical definition of the Caribbean that we shall adopt, and in the context of which the Anglophone countries will be discussed, is that of the "semienclosed sea," whose "geographical heartland is contained in the north by the Greater Antilles (Cuba, Hispaniola, Puerto Rico); on the east by the Lesser Antilles, including Barbados; by the shores of Colombia, Venezuela, and Panama to the South; and by Central America and Yucatan Mexico to the west."[2] But as we have indicated, consideration must be given, in dealing with the interests of various *political* entities, to some countries that, strictly speaking, exist on the periphery of this heartland. Of these, the Bahamas, for example, constitute the only archipelagic entity organized as a single political jurisdiction, at a time when the underdeveloped states constituted as archipelagoes have made specific demands within the UNCLOS III framework. Discussions of the Bahamas' entitlement to archipelagic status before the independence of that country in 1973 were dominated by the United Kingdom.[3]

## Characteristics and context of existence of the states

The archipelago states of CARICOM are dwarfed in physical size by most of the other continental states bordering the Caribbean, and indeed by the older archipelago states of the Greater Antilles (Cuba, Haiti, and the Dominican Republic). The largest of the CARICOM states, Jamaica (4,410 sq. mi.), is less than half the physical size of the Haitian Republic (10,700 sq. mi.). The small physical sizes are, in general, also reflected in shorelines that are, relatively, not of great length. There is, however, a greater relative equality between the two sets of countries in terms of their national income as reflected by gross national product indexes.

The small size of the states is not compensated for by the kind of pooled resources and collective objectives about the utilization of the resources of the area that might derive from their falling under a single political jurisdiction. The effort at federation was short lived. And it might in fact be suggested that the effective implementation of an arrangement such as a *mare clausum* for the area would indeed require more coherent political arrangements than the existing institutional linkages between these states. Thus, efforts by the Trinidad and Tobago government in 1973 to pursue Caribbean-wide discussions to find a regime for the Caribbean were not successful.

This is not to say that the implications of an archipelagic status for these states would have been welcomed by greater powers in the area. As is known, no agreement about archipelagoes was arrived at during the 1958 Geneva Conference on the Law of the Sea. The resulting convention is silent on the issue. Remarks made after the conference by the chairman of the U.S. delegation hinted at potential difficulties envisaged at that time:

> If the Philippine and Indonesian claims . . . that the waters "around, between and connecting" the islands of an archipelago should be treated as internal waters and the surrounding areas, determined from straight base lines, treated as territorial waters were accepted, the whole of the South Eastern Pacific would be removed from high seas as would other areas such as the Federation of the West Indies in the Caribbean.
>
> The harmful effects of any such extension on sea navigation would be great and the effects on air navigation might be catastrophic.[4]

The evolution in thinking about a regime for archipelagoes is reflected in the current UNCLOS III Negotiating Text, which insists, of course, that the entities should fall under a single jurisdiction.

As islands, the states of the Caribbean archipelago differ from other underdeveloped island-states in the contemporary world. They do not, as is the case of many of the island-states of the Pacific, suffer from the presumed economic disadvantages of remoteness from continental mainlands. But neither do they have the wide-open sea spaces surrounding them (and therefore the entitlement to expansive exclusive economic or fisheries zones).

Existing as they do in a semienclosed sea, most of the states are "zone-locked," the extreme case being Jamaica, which has adopted the nomenclature of being "Carib-locked."[5] Along with the other Greater Antilles, Jamaica has therefore claimed the status of being a geographically disadvantaged state. On the other hand, given the length of the Caribbean coastlines and their locations, the rimland states of Venezuela and Colombia can bring large expanses under economic-zone jurisdiction and give themselves a presence in the Caribbean Sea that dominates that of the archipelago states. In their perceptions of the gains that can be derived from their locations in this respect,

Venezuela and Colombia appear to have more in common with Guyana than the latter has with the other states of CARICOM, of which it is a member.

From a geopolitical point of view the archipelago states lie in the shadow of the major military and maritime power in the region, the United States, which asserts, by virtue of size and power, certain entitlements in the Caribbean Sea based on claimed responsibilities for global order. This assertion implies that in terms of international *politics* the states of the archipelago constitute a subordinate system (de facto) within a U.S.-dominated system, against whose interests the archipelago states' interests must be asserted. As often noted, the archipelago is the locus of a number of sea-lanes considered important to U.S. economic and strategic security. Finally, as with many other small island-states, tourism has become an important financial resource for many of the countries. In the words of a Bahamian delegate to UNCLOS III a large proportion of their earnings depends "on the clearness of the waters and the cleanness of the beaches."[6] This need gives the states in question a major interest in the matters of pollution and preservation of the marine environment. Trinidad and Tobago, both as a petroleum-producing country and as a locus of tourism facilities, sees itself as "both a potential polluter of the marine environment and a victim of its consequences."[7]

## Caribbean-related U.S. interests

Given the global predominance of the United States, its Caribbean interests might be said to fall into two classes, general and specific. Since the Caribbean functions, in effect, as an important link between North and South America and between the Pacific and Atlantic coasts of the United States, it represents for the United States an instance of the important legal principles of unencumbered access and transit through routes deemed necessary for international navigation. There are a number of important passages between the various islands of the Caribbean, a sufficient number of which, as Osgood has observed, are wider than 25 miles and therefore not affected by the generally accepted 12-mile limit of territorial waters. Writing in 1974, Osgood was concerned to stress that restrictions on passage and overflight might pose greater impediments to the mobility of the U.S. general purpose military forces than to American nuclear strategic capability.[8] But the general principle of access speaks to both economic and military concerns.

U.S. concern with the significance and activity of Cuba in the hemisphere has also given rise to concern that the Soviet Union should not have too great a presence in the area of the Caribbean Sea. Such expressions take varying forms of sophistication, from the view that "the Caribbean is turning into a

Soviet lake" to reasonably precise analyses of the varieties of U.S. presences in the area.[9]

There is also an American concern with access to the class of semienclosed seas, of which the Caribbean is one of an estimated twenty-five throughout the globe. There has been increasing cognizance of the desire of the countries encompassed by such seas to exert prior claim on their resources as well as to ensure the sustenance of their ecological characteristics. On the other hand, it is argued that, given their importance, "the rights of the international community as a whole to access to these waters" must be ensured by any protective regime.[10] The United States, therefore, has a general interest in broadly applicable principles in respect to semienclosed seas.

More specific U.S. interests in the Caribbean concern the protection of a variety of economic investments in the area's countries, her dependence on the area's production of certain critical raw materials such as bauxite, and maintenance of access to channels that serve both her commercial and her military traffic through the Panama Canal, around the northeastern Atlantic, and through the Yucatan Channel and Bahamian-encompassed waters.[11] In addition, the United States is physically represented in the "geographical heartland" through her jurisdiction over Puerto Rico and the U.S. Virgin Islands and a network of monitoring and submarine devices designed to enhance her security. The possession of colonies and associated states in the Caribbean takes the United States fully into the process of boundary delimitation vis-à-vis other archipelagic and continental Caribbean states.

As developments during the course of UNCLOS III have indicated, this variety of interests is subject to the push and pull of interest-group pressure in the United States. Such pressures have produced the extension of the fishery zone of the United States to 200 miles (forcing other countries—the Bahamas and Cuba—to respond) and have resulted in congressional legislation on deep sea bed mining. Kissinger, as secretary of state, suggested in a speech largely devoted to these matters, the essential justification:

> The United States cannot indefinitely sacrifice its own interest in developing an assured supply of critical resources to an indefinitely prolonged negotiation. . . . The United States cannot indefinitely accept unregulated and indiscriminate foreign fishing off its coasts.[12]

In summary, then, the interests of the United States in the Caribbean can be said to be fairly representative of its general Law of the Sea interests. The disparity in size and power between it and many of the Caribbean countries might suggest that they would have a broad interest in alliance with other, more substantial Third World countries in the protection of their own interests vis-à-vis the United States.

## Caribbean-related interests of other rimland countries

Reference here is mainly to Venezuela and Colombia, though it needs also to be made to the relationship between Mexico and the northern Caribbean and between Brazil on the geographical periphery of the Caribbean and certain Caribbean countries.

### *Venezuela*

As her representatives have often claimed, partly in the face of opposition to her assertion of interests, the 3,000-km. Venezuelan coastline on the Caribbean is the longest of any Caribbean country. It has often been pointed out that important commercial and industrial centers of Venezuela such as Caracas and Maracaibo face the Caribbean and that the Caribbean outlet is of prime significance to the Venezuelan export of oil and oil products, the major source of the country's foreign exchange. Reference is often also made to the difference between Colombia and Venezuela; both are Caribbean and Andean countries, but the Colombian capital faces in an Andean direction while Venezuela's faces the Caribbean. "Venezuelan history," President Andres Perez said at the opening of UNCLOS III, "had developed along the Caribbean and largely under its influence," but, on the other hand, "the country had never applied a policy toward the sea." In recent years just such a policy became fairly explicit. Venezuela has "firmly advocated the concept of the patrimonial sea"[13] and has moved to initiate a series of boundary delimitations and fisheries agreements with other Caribbean and Caribbean-related countries.

In addition to Venezuela's Caribbean presence deriving from the extent of its coastline, two other aspects of its Law of the Sea behavior are noteworthy. The first is the historical delimitation treaty between the United Kingdom and Venezuela concerning the Gulf of Paria, now in effect a treaty between Venezuela and Trinidad and Tobago—an arrangement delimiting submarine areas of this semienclosed sea.[14] The second aspect relates to Venezuelan possession of Aves Island in the northern Caribbean and the resulting implications in light of the fact that consensus was developing that islands, properly defined, might be entitled to their own Law of the Sea regime. To Caribbean countries, Venezuela's presence in the area would thus appear in a different perspective.

Venezuela had designated 1973 as the "Year of Maritime Assertion."[15] As is now well known, her subsequent activities or claims in respect to the Caribbean proved disconcerting to the archipelagic country with whom she has had the tightest relationships, Trinidad and Tobago. The prime minister of that country has suggested that Venezuela seeks an overbearing influence in the Caribbean and that her past record indicates an incapability to resolve her boundary claims in a definitive fashion. Venezuela's continuing difficulties with Colombia, her claim over Guyanese territory (which would have sea delimitation implications), and her persistent difficulties with Trinidad over fisheries in particular are all brought into play in support of the claim of Venezuelan search for influence and Venezuelan intransigence.[16]

Whatever the rights and wrongs of the various assertions and counter-assertions, it can fairly be said that Venezuela has an integral presence in the Caribbean Sea, in relation to which (as in the case of the United States) the CARICOM countries have, of necessity, to match and measure their own claims and interests.

*Colombia*

As hinted, Colombia has been in continuous dispute with Venezuela over boundary delimitation. Some of Colombia's observations on the status of islands, at UNCLOS III, appear to be made in obvious reference to its problems with Venezuela.[17] But Colombia has difficulties with Nicaragua in the northwestern Caribbean.

For purposes here, however, it is the implications of Colombia's patrimonial sea or exclusive economic zone extensions that are of concern since they have posed potential problems, for Jamaican fishing interests in particular. The Jamaican minister responsible for Law of the Sea matters observed at the opening of the UNCLOS III sessions in Venezuela in 1974 that, even acknowledging its legitimacy, the patrimonial sea concept should not be "applied so rigidly as to cut off the source of livelihood of fishermen long established in a particular area."[18] And Jamaica has been attempting since the early 1970s to establish agreements with Colombia in particular: Jamaica had originally been concerned to negotiate fishing rights in the territorial waters of Colombia, but the problem will be exacerbated by virtual international agreement on the exclusive economic zone.[19] Unlike Cuba, for example, Jamaica's fishing industry is a small-craft rather than a deep-sea operation.

*Mexico*

The Caribbean coastline of Mexico is only one, and a limited one, of her coastline interests, including as they do also the Gulf of Mexico, the Pacific, and the Gulf of California. A nexus of relationships is increasingly developing in the northwestern tier of the Caribbean, involving fisheries, the legal and illegal movement of persons, and the illegal movement of drugs, encompassing Mexico, the United States, Cuba, Hispaniola, Jamaica, and the Bahamas. With regard to fisheries, Mexico, which has favored preferential fishing zones, has agreed to a series of bilateral arrangements with interested countries. In the Caribbean, Cuba has been the country involved, given its extensive fishing industry.[20] The possibility clearly exists that Jamaica, if it developed the capacity for a deep-sea fishing industry, would wish to reach similar agreements. Mexico has taken the position that it has become necessary to correct the historical situation in which "freedom of fishing had favored the great Powers at the expense of the small," but it indicated a sensitivity to "the situation of the Caribbean States, whose problems would not be solved by the establishment of patrimonial seas."[21]

### *Brazil*

Given the relative paucity of the Caribbean Sea waters with respect to fisheries, CARICOM countries such as Barbados and Trinidad and Tobago have sought to reach agreements with Brazil. Originally Brazil had asserted a 200-mile territorial waters zone, but it has compromised on the consensus solution of the exclusive economic zone. Brazil signed separate shrimping agreements with Barbados and Trinidad in February 1975, although the operationalization of these has not been particularly satisfactory. Guyana has followed Brazil in asserting jurisdiction over a 200-mile zone for the protection of fisheries resources. This has led to difficulties with some smaller CARICOM countries such as St. Lucia, which have sought more concessionary arrangements than those that Guyana would normally sign with larger powers.

In summary, a statement on the Caribbean-related interests of the United States and the rimland countries: at the same time that political fragmentation of the archipelago is occurring, the CARICOM states do not appear to have an "integrity" that would facilitate protection of their interests as small states. It is against this background that the positions and interests of these states in the UNCLOS III environment must be examined.

## The positions of the CARICOM countries

In the course of making his critical remarks on Venezuela in 1975, the prime minister of Trinidad referred to "the overwhelming disaster facing us—the CARICOM states—in respect of the pending new international agreements on the Law of the Sea," and he called for a "common Caribbean position on the Law of the Sea aimed specifically at securing international recognition for a special regime for the Caribbean multigovernmental archipelago." Later in the same year, opening the Western Central Atlantic Fisheries Commission, he asserted that extensions of 200-mile fisheries or exclusive economic zones would "be catastrophic for Caribbean countries that are in a state of virtual dependency on access to fisheries resources of the Western Central Atlantic region."[22]

Prime Minister Williams sought to find some appropriate institutional framework in which the interests and objectives of the archipelago states might be concerted. The CARICOM framework was insufficiently inclusive to accommodate the non-Anglophone states. He was inclined to make use of the newly organized Caribbean Development Cooperation Committee of the Economic Commission for Latin America (ECLA), since this included all the archipelagic countries, Guyana and Surinam but not Venezuela, and the rimland countries.

Clearly the all-embracing regional approach of the 1972 Declaration of Santo Domingo was not satisfactory, though it had been the culmination of previous preparatory meetings. Trinidad, though it signed the declaration proposing a patrimonial sea of 200 nautical miles, did have some qualifications about its implementation in the Caribbean. Barbados, Guyana, and Jamaica did not sign, though the proposal might be said to serve the interests of Guyana.[23]

The Declaration of Santo Domingo, though composed by Caribbean Basin states (including El Salvador but excluding Cuba), can really be said to have served the main interests of the larger rimland countries of Spanish heritage. It reinforced their insistence, begun in the 1940s, on jurisdiction over expansive sea areas. In that sense, the declaration, though emanating from a conference of Caribbean countries and as a Caribbean doctrine, basically reinforced the South American position. Castañeda has rightly argued that

> the Santo Domingo Declaration . . . was not an answer of the Caribbean countries to a regional problem. We did not meet there in order to find a legal answer to the problem of the Caribbean. . . . In fact, it has very little to do with it. What is more, the fact that all the participants were Caribbean countries was almost circumstantial. What was intended was to try to reach agreement on what could become a proposal for one aspect of a worldwide legal regime.
>
> Why is this so? The Caribbean, because of its very nature, lends itself very little to this kind of regime or solution called the patrimonial sea.[24]

In essence, although a certain amount of diplomatic cooperation has taken place and the CARICOM countries have been participants in international and subregional organizations concerned with scientific research, pollution, and the marine environment, no substantial advance has been made toward elaborating a *regional* solution. A review of legislation implemented in respect to each island's particular interests in response to global developments is given by Menon.[25]

We need to examine the expressions by the CARICOM countries of their maritime interests as evidenced in the documentation of UNCLOS III, especially the early stages of the conference. Trinidad has been involved in the preparatory arrangements for UNCLOS III and, with Jamaica, Guyana, and to a lesser extent Barbados, has played a fairly active part in the proceedings of the conference. The Bahamas moved quickly after independence to assert its special claims for an archipelagic status, obviously having common interests with active countries such as Indonesia, the Philippines, and Fiji but seeking to have the conference recognize her distinct characteristics. Grenada appears to have played little part in the conference after independence in 1974; Dominica, St. Lucia, and St. Vincent obtained their independence toward the end of the 1970s, when for the most part solutions, for example, on the status of islands, were already beginning to gel.

Though there is substantial CARICOM interest and input in the proceedings of the three main conference committees, we might hazard the suggestion that the major concerns with their particular interests lay in the Second Committee, which was engaged with questions relating to the territorial sea, exclusive economic zone (EEZ), continental shelf, islands, archipelagoes, and attendant issues of rights of passage. This is not to say that there has not been a serious concern with Third Committee issues of marine environment preservation, pollution, and the transfer of technology. And the issue of the seabed regime has an importance for all Group of 77 countries as well as having for Jamaica the special interest of seeking to provide the site for the proposed International Seabed Authority.

On the question of the regime for the seabed beyond the limits of national jurisdiction, the CARICOM countries joined other Third World countries in adhering to the notion of the "common heritage of mankind," favoring the notion that an important role in this area should be given to an international authority while conceding, in the words of the Jamaican delegate, that "the problem was how to reconcile the interests of those whose heritage the area was and the interests of those who had the necessary technology to exploit the area."[26] This problem would continue to haunt the progress of the conference, with the United States and other countries rejecting at the seventh session (1978) the formula contained in the Informal Composite Negotiating Text

(ICNT).[27] At the 1974 Caracas session, Trinidad and Tobago took essentially the same position as that of Jamaica.

An interesting set of position statements came out of the 1974 sessions of the Second Committee. In general, we perceive an interest on the part of Trinidad and Tobago in issues relating to the continental shelf, exclusive economic zone, and the rights of islands—this last reflecting a certain concern with protecting the rights of the still-dependent West Indies Associated States. Jamaica's constant concern was her status as a zone-locked state and, therefore, the rights of geographically disadvantaged states (which, with the land-locked states, constituted a third of the membership of a conference reaching decisions by consensus). Barbados wanted to require protection for small island-states with short coastlines and without the privilege of extensive continental shelves. The Bahamas was concerned with finding a meaningful recognition of her archipelagic status. All countries supported the evolved consensus on a 12-mile territorial sea, though some were concerned to link such support to the conference's acceptance of other claims of concern to the Caribbean region. Trinidad's position is indicative of this:

> She supported the 12-nautical mile limit for the territorial sea, provided, however, an exclusive economic zone was accepted, and the concept of the continental shelf was retained. As her delegation had stated at the twenty-third plenary meeting, it saw an organic link between the territorial sea, the exclusive economic zone, and regional or other arrangements concerning *preferential* rights of access to the exclusive economic zones and zones of national jurisdiction.[28]

Jamaica's position was, in principle, a little more rigid:

> Jamaica did not support the concept of the economic zone or the patrimonial sea or sovereign territorial zones beyond 12 miles, but as a compromise it was prepared to accept the establishment of such zones provided that right of access was granted to the geographically disadvantaged developing countries.[29]

Stressing on another occasion the necessity for the conference "to create a legal order which did not necessarily reflect the accidents of geography," the Jamaican delegate drew attention to his delegation's proposal for a document stressing the "rights of developing geographically disadvantaged states" defined as states which

> were land-locked or for geographical, biological, or ecological reasons derived no substantial economic advantage from establishing an economic zone or patrimonial sea; or States which were adversely affected in their economies by the establishment of economic zones or patrimonial seas of other States; or States which had short coastlines and could not extend uniformly their national jurisdiction.[30]

Cuba held a position not dissimilar from that of the CARICOM countries, based on the view that the "geographical situation of Cuba prevented it from having a wide territorial sea or a uniform economic zone." Reflecting her interests as a deep-sea fishing nation, the Cuban delegate argued that "many coastal States would not be able fully to exploit the fish resources in their zone and should therefore allow other States to enter the area, on a discriminatory basis."[31] Cuba has established bilateral agreements with a number of countries—both developed and underdeveloped—although her president has recently argued that "the establishment of a 200-mile limit for territorial waters and the abrogation of some fishing agreements placed limits on our high seas fishing fleet."[32]

Guyana seemed irritated with the stress on *preferential* rights for disadvantaged states, for in discussing the exclusive economic zone, her delegate made reference to

> the introduction of outrageous qualifications which were postulated as prior conditions to the acceptance of that [EEZ] doctrine by certain States. The most untenable of those qualifications pertained to the recognition of a right of access by other States to the living resources in the exclusive economic zone of a coastal State which might temporarily be incapable of fully exploiting those resources.[33]

This position is akin to that expressed by the South American countries, including Guyana's neighbor Brazil, whose representative resisted the idea that "the rights of the coastal State in the economic zone should be defined in narrower terms than those admitted in the continental shelf."[34]

Even Trinidad has appeared hesitant at times to accept the drive to attain maximum concessions by the geographically disadvantaged states. In discussing the continental shelf, her delegate found it necessary to indicate that there was no reason why all states should be equally endowed with the same characteristics:

> the absence of a continental shelf in certain States had redounded to their benefit in that they were endowed with fine natural harbours and unspoilt beaches, and, in certain cases, with fertile fishing grounds.[35]

In relation to the issue of *archipelagoes*, the Bahamas noted its particular characteristics:

> The entire area of land and sea over which the Bahamas claimed jurisdiction was approximately 100,000 square miles, approximately 94 percent of which was sea, forming an intrinsic geographical entity and constituting an almost perfect archipelago, *traversed by heavily trafficked shipping* lanes. . . . The special problem of archipelagoes was that the sea-lanes which threaded them had some of the characteristics of international straits.[36]

Again,

> The Bahama Banks presented a special problem of delimitation since both the ratio of very shallow water to dry-land areas and the steepness of the slopes appeared to be unparalleled. . . . The length-of-baseline criteria became irrelevant when applied to the unique circumstances of the Bahama Islands and Banks.[37]

The Bahamas proposed its own draft article on archipelagic states.[38]

It appears from comments of various delegates, particularly those of the United States, concerned with the principle of transit that the draft Part IV on Archipelagic States in the ICNT prepared for the ninth session is satisfactory to those involved. The articles define the concept of "archipelagic waters" and speak to the question of the regime of archipelagic sea-lanes passage.[39] One academic analyst has argued that "archipelagoes have played the straits game and have neglected the battle for the archipelago principle. UNCLOS III has failed to deal with the archipelago principle as a sea-centered concept."[40] Nonetheless, given the major powers' deep interest in this question, the result appears to be an acceptable compromise, and the development of the EEZ concept appears to have provided a mechanism for minimizing the problem of archipelagic jurisdiction over wide expanses of ocean. The integral nature of the solutions arrived at is suggested in a statement by an American participant:

> The acceptability of the concept and the precision of its elaboration were at the outset and remain largely one and the same issue. Thus, it is not clear whether states that are prepared to accept the ICNT provisions on archipelagic states as part of an overall generally acceptable law of the sea treaty would be prepared to recognize the archipelago concept in the absence of such a treaty.[41]

Finally, the issue of *islands* gave rise to some muted disputation. It will be recalled that Prime Minister Williams was concerned with the implications of Venezuelan ownership and jurisdiction over Aves Island and the northeastern Caribbean. Some Caribbean countries will have seen that the U.S. decision to negotiate bilateral agreements with Venezuela entailing delimitations in the Caribbean Sea, in particular extending the productivity of an EEZ for Aves Island, will have the potential consequence of involving a net loss for countries like Dominica and St. Kitts, which have traditionally fished in that area. Trinidad, however, in the early sessions of the conference, was more concerned to protect the interests of the nonsovereign Anglophone states of the Caribbean Community. Its delegate observed that

> in the Sea-bed Committee his delegation had rejected proposals aimed at establishing a regime that sought to curtail the jurisdiction and sovereignty of islands over the ocean space adjacent to their coasts. . . . The only relevant question was whether islands under colonial dependence or foreign domination or control were entitled to the breadth of territorial sea, exclusive economic zone, continental shelf rights, and the jurisdiction to be established by the conference in a new convention on the law of the sea. His delegation believed that they were entitled to those rights. . . .
>
> The associated States and other colonial territories of the Caribbean, although not yet fully independent, were self-governing entities responsible for the welfare of their peoples. They were legitimately entitled to the same rights and benefits in ocean space as were to be accorded to continental States in any new convention of the law of the sea. . . .
>
> His delegation was not referring to uninhabited rocks and cays in the middle of the seas and oceans that were under foreign domination or control.[42]

Cuba, concerned with the question of U.S. jurisdiction over Puerto Rico, took a different view in order to inhibit what it perceived to be the extension of U.S. jurisdiction in the Caribbean. Cuba linked this to the possibilities of industrial pollution from the United States.

We should note, in the context of Colombia's difficulties with Venezuela, the Colombian delegate's expressed fear that the definition of "island" could lead to a situation in which "any minor elevation could call itself an island."[43]

The question of the preservation of the marine environment, the province of the Third Committee, indicated that the Caribbean states, especially those concerned with tourism, had an ambivalence characteristic of many other Group of 77 states. It is summarized in the statement from the delegate of Barbados:

> The island of Barbados, because of its geographical situation, was particularly vulnerable to the effects of pollution arising in the mid-Atlantic. . . . The alarming levels of pollution in the mid-Atlantic constituted a potentially serious threat to the fisheries and tourist industry of the island. . . . While recognizing that weak measures were pointless, Barbados, as a developing country, could not be party to standards so high that they impeded its industrial development or that of other States of the third world.[44]

## Conclusion

What gains can be said to have been made by the CARICOM countries from the ongoing UNCLOS III? If countries were hoping for a framework that might have assisted in the formation of a regional arrangement that could give relatively equal access to all constituent members, it was not achieved. Reflecting some of her geographical characteristics defined as deficiencies, the Jamaican suggestion of a "matrimonial sea" arrangement for the Caribbean never received much support, either from the conference as a whole or from members of the Group of 77. The traditional, strongly geopolitically centered approach of the Central American states in particular militates against the development of a coherent, collective regime for the area.

Although there appears to be increased regional and international sensitivity to the types of geographical disadvantages in respect to access to the resources of the sea, it does not appear that this sensitivity has as yet brought substantial material advantage. In some cases coastal states such as Mexico and Brazil have granted concessionary terms to other deprived states. But these imply no suggestion of "preferentiality." It has, in fact, been claimed for UNCLOS III so far, not that it creates a framework for privileged arrangements but rather that it permits the development of normal bilateral and multilateral agreements within some framework of global consensus.

The network of Caribbean Community relationships has not developed to the extent that a member country such as Guyana might perceive the exploitation of its resources in its exclusive economic zone as susceptible to becoming part of a system of tradeoffs within a Caribbean multilateral framework. In a sense, there needs to be a larger mix of total resources of various kinds than is available within the present CARICOM system. This might imply the participation of rimland countries like Venezuela and Colombia. But no framework, with the exception of the functionally specific one of the Caribbean Development Bank, presently exists to encompass these countries.

Finally, it might be noted that Jamaica was able to utilize the sets of relationships developed during the 1970s in the Group of 77 and the nonaligned movement to garner support for its offer of a site for the proposed International Seabed Authority. This offer is undoubtedly directed to the further development of the country's tourism industry and its development as a recognized conference center. Assuming that the bias in her favor stands within UNCLOS III, this will be one example of the beneficial results deriving from the integration of certain types of external relations activities over a number of issue areas and in varying institutional contexts.

## Notes

1. *See generally* F.V. GARCÍA-AMADOR, *The Latin American Contribution to the Development of the Law of the Sea*, 68 AM. J. INT'L L. 33–50 (1974).

2. R. D. HODGSON, *The American Mediterranean: One Sea, One Region?* in GULF AND CARIBBEAN MARITIME PROBLEMS 7 (L. Alexander ed. 1973). The sovereign states of the archipelagic Caribbean are The Bahamas, Jamaica, Barbados, Dominica, St. Lucia, St. Vincent, Grenada, Trinidad and Tobago, and Guyana.

3. *See* D. P. O'CONNELL, *Mid-Ocean Archipelagoes in International Law*, 45 BRIT. Y. B. INT'L L. 2, 51–53, 56–57 (1971). The archipelago principle can in fact be applied to multi-island states such as Trinidad and Tobago, Grenada, St. Vincent and the Grenadines, and Antigua.

4. ARTHUR H. DEAN, *The Geneva Conference on the Law of the Sea: What Was Accomplished?* 52 AM. J. INT'L L. 611–12 at n.14 (1958).

5. *See* K. O. RATTRAY, A. KIRTON, AND P. ROBINSON, *The Effect of the Existing Law of the Sea on the Development of the Caribbean Region and the Gulf of Mexico*, in

PACEM IN MARIBUS: CARIBBEAN STUDY AND DIALOGUE 256–57 (E. Borgese ed. 1974).

6. 1 Third United Nations Conference on the Law of the Sea, Official Records, plen. mtgs., 1st sess., 33d mtg. 132, para. 66 (1975), UN Sales no. E.75.V.3 (hereinafter cited as UNCLOS OR).

7. 2 UNCLOS OR, Summary Records of 3d Comm., 4th mtg. 321, para. 71, UN Sales no. E.75.V.4.

8. R. OSGOOD, *U.S. Security Interests in Ocean Law*, 2 OCEAN DEV. & INT'L L. 5–36 (1974).

9. For the quoted remarks, *see* Congressman Bill Chappell of Florida, *The Caribbean Sea*, 16 VITAL SPEECHES OF THE DAY 689 (1980). For a more sophisticated analysis, see MARGARET D. HAYES, *Security to the South: U.S. Interests in Latin America*, 5 INT'L SECURITY 130–51 (1980).

10. LEWIS M. ALEXANDER, *Regionalism and the Law of the Sea: The Case of Semi-Enclosed Seas*, 2 OCEAN DEV. & INT'L L. 151–86 (1974).

11. *See* HAYES, *supra* note 9, for a summary.

12. HENRY KISSINGER, *International Law, World Order and Human Progress*, speech delivered on 11 August 1975 before the Annual Convention of the American Bar Assn., reproduced in 73 BULLETIN, Dept. of State, 353–62 (1975).

13. Address by President Carlos Andres Perez, 1 UNCLOS OR, 14th mtg. 37, para. 30.

14. *See* on these matters and on what follows two articles by Kaldone G. Nweihed: *"EZ" (Uneasy) Delimitation in the Semi-Enclosed Caribbean Sea: Recent Agreements between Venezuela and Her Neighbors*, 8 OCEAN DEV. & INT'L L. 1–33 (1980); and *infra* note 15.

15. KALDONE G. NWEIHED, *Venezuela's Contribution to the Contemporary Law of the Sea*, 11 SAN DIEGO L. REV. 603–33 (1974), at 603.

16. *See* ERIC WILLIAMS, *The Threat to the Caribbean Community*, speech of 15 June 1975, reproduced in 1975 CARIBBEAN Y. B. OF INT'L REL. 586–606 (1976).

17. 2 UNCLOS OR, 2d Comm., 39th mtg. 280–81, paras. 13–21. *See also* ROBERT D. KLOCK, *Gulf of Venezuela: A Proposed Delimitation*, 12 LAWYER OF THE AMERICAS 93–108 (1980).

18. 1 UNCLOS OR, 27th mtg. 98, para. 27.

19. *See infra* pp. 8–16.

20. J. E. CARROZ AND M. J. SAVINI, *The New International Law of Fisheries Emerging from Bilateral Agreements*, 3 MARINE POLICY 79–98 (1979).

21. Address by President Luis Echeverría Alvarez, I UNCLOS OR, 45th mtg. 196, para. 9; 197, para. 25.

22. WILLIAMS, *supra* note 16, at 601; and *200-mile Fisheries Zone Would be Catastrophic for Caribbean Countries*, Jamaica Daily News, 24 October 1975 at 1. *See also* LENNOX F. BALLAH, *Applicability of the Archipelago and Mare Clausum Concepts to the Caribbean Sea*, in PACEM IN MARIBUS, *supra* note 5, at 276–304.

23. *Specialized Conference of Caribbean Countries Concerning the Problems of the Sea: Declaration of Santo Domingo, June 9, 1972*, reproduced in 11 INT'L LEGAL

MATERIALS, 892–93 (1972). *See also Guyana Wants 200-Mile Zone*. Trinidad Guardian, 26 March 1974 at 8.

24. *See* PROCEEDINGS: PACEM IN MARIBUS IV 115 (D. Kreigel ed. 1974).

25. P. K. MENON, *The Commonwealth Caribbean and the Development of the Sea: An Overview*, REVUE DE DROIT INTERNATIONAL 39–74 (1980). For their involvement with other Caribbean countries in scientific and related questions, *see* J. F. PULVENIS, *La Mer des Caraïbes*, 84 REVUE GENERALE DE DROIT INTERNATIONAL PUBLIC 310–27 (1980).

26. 2 UNCLOS OR, 1st Comm., 11th mtg. 58, para. 69.

27. For justification, *see* BERNARD H. OXMAN, *The Third United Nations Conference on the Law of the Sea: The Seventh Session (1978)*, 73 AM. J. INTL'L L. 1–41 (1979). This article contains the relevant portion of Ambassador Richardson's statement at 35, n. 119.

28. 2 UNCLOS OR, 2d Comm., 7th mtg. 118, para. 5 (emphasis added).

29. *Id.*, 5th mtg. 111, para. 29.

30. *Id.*, 2d Comm., 28th mtg. 219, para. 28. The document to which the Jamaican delegate referred was the joint proposal by Haiti and Jamaica on "the rights of developing geographically disadvantaged States within the economic zone or patrimonial sea." *See* Doc. A/Conf.62/C.2/L.35 in 3 UNCLOS OR, DOCUMENTS OF THE CONFERENCE, at 213 (1975), UN Sales no. E.75.V.5.

31. 2 UNCLOS OR, 2d Comm., 4th mtg. 104, para. 9.

32. *See Special Supplement on the Cuban Fishing Industry*, GRANMA WEEKLY REVIEW, 15 February 1981, at 1.

33. 2 UNCLOS OR, 2d Comm., 26 mtg. 208, para. 73.

34. *Id.*, 2d Comm., 26th mtg. 202, para. 5.

35. *Id.*, 2d Comm., 18th mtg. 154, para. 85.

36. 1 *id.*, plen. mtgs., 33d mtg. 132, paras. 60–63 (emphasis added).

37. 2 *id.*, 2d Comm., 36th mtg. 265, paras. 77–79.

38. Doc. A/Conf.62/C.2/L.70 in 3 *id.*, at 236.

39. DRAFT CONVENTION ON THE LAW OF THE SEA (INFORMAL TEXT), UN Doc. A/Conf.62/WP.10/Rev.3 and UN Doc. A/Conf.62/WP.10/Rev.3/Corr.1, reproduced in 19 INT'L LEGAL MATERIALS 1129 (1980) at 1159–62.

40. DALE ANDREW, *Archipelagoes and the Law of the Sea*, 2 MARINE POLICY 46–64 (1978).

41. BERNARD H. OXMAN, *The Third United Nations Conference on the Law of the Sea: The 1977 New York Session*, 72 AM. J. INT'L L. 66 (1978).

42. 2 UNCLOS OR, 2d Comm., 39th mtg. 282, paras. 42–46.

43. *Id.*, 2d Comm., 39th mtg. 280, para. 17. *See*, however, Article 121 of the ICNT, REPRODUCED IN 16 INT'L LEGAL MATERIALS 1152 (1977).

44. *Id.*, 3d Comm., 6th mtg. 332, paras. 57–58.

# Delimitation Principles and Problems in the Caribbean

*Kaldone G. Nweihed*

DELIMITATION OF maritime space is the direct outcome of two obvious situations: the contiguity and the multiplicity of political sovereignties within the area in common. The first situation becomes evident in semienclosed seas as distinct from continental coasts on open ocean space; the second is the result of complex historical processes in which economics, geopolitics, strategy, social relations, and other factors are involved. There is no geographic area in the world that offers a clearer combination of both situations than the inter-American Mediterranean, or the joint area of the Greater Caribbean and the Gulf of Mexico. The Sea of Okhotsk, for instance, is geographically a more perfect semienclosed sea than the Caribbean, but it lacks the historical process; the Sunda Seas (Java, Banda, Molucca) have had a simple historical process which has determined their appurtenance to one main social group, the State of Indonesia.

Delimitation of maritime boundaries constitutes one of the most complex issues in the emerging Law of the Sea. As the need arose to define and characterize the distinct maritime areas under national jurisdiction, so did the corollary exigency of fixing their limits.

Literature on the delimitation of maritime boundaries is relatively scarce compared to the amount available on other aspects of the Law of the Sea. Besides the articles contained in the 1958 Geneva Conventions on the Law of the Sea and the text of the draft Law of the Sea Convention (September 1980), which, it is hoped, will be converted into the Caracas Convention on the Law of the Sea, the other main sources on which the investigator draws are jurisprudence and state practice. [The Law of the Sea Treaty was signed in Jamaica on 10 December 1982.—Ed.] The recommended method is the inductive: individual cases are studied on their own merits, and certain principles and methods are singled out for later comparison and classification. In quantitative terms, considering the sum of potential maritime delimitations around the globe, the process is just starting; in qualitative terms, however, the world community already enjoys the benefit of several test cases and numerous examples of successful maritime delimitation completed in delicate areas and at reasonable cost.[1]

A systematic examination of maritime delimitation agreements will reveal two distinct types of information, which correspondingly call for a dual classification: the first based on the legal nature of the offshore or seaward areas to be delimited, and the second upon the principle of delimitation and the method employed. Both levels will be discussed briefly, as will be the establishment of straight baselines for the measurement of territorial seas because of the intimate relationship of this method of demarcating baselines with the concept of delimitation.

## The legal nature of the offshore areas

During the early fifties, prior to the Geneva Conference, there was still much confusion about the maritime provinces enclosed in seaward areas under national jurisdiction that could be delimited among riparian states. During the three decades between the 1930 Hague Conference and the coming into force of the Geneva regime in the sixties, the main concern was the lateral delimitation of the territorial sea and of "any contiguous zone, or zones," as Professor Boggs said. The term in plural was meant to cover seaward parallel belts coterminous on the landward side with the outer limit of the territorial sea, including the by-then-emerging contiguous zone proper and any other belts created for other purposes such as fishery conservation (Vietnam, 20 km., 1936),[2] security (Italy, 10 n.m., 1912),[3] and pollution control (Portugal, 6 n.m., 1928).[4] Nevertheless, delimitation in general did not weigh as a pressing issue in those days, unless there was a particularly delicate dispute that could be solved only on the basis of prior determination and subsequent demarcation of boundaries.

Hodgson and Smith observed that "before World War II, few state boundaries existed in the waters adjacent to continental masses. Typical ones were established by the Norwegian-Swedish Boundary Agreements of 1661, 1897, 1904, and 1909 and the Finno-Swedish Agreement of 1811. . . . The first extensive sea boundary was created in 1942 when the United Kingdom and Venezuela delimited a continental shelf boundary in the Gulf of Paria between Trinidad and the South American mainland; the boundary extended beyond the territorial sea claim of either state."[5]

Hardly three decades had elapsed since the Paria Treaty, with quite a number of continental shelves already delimited between opposite and adjacent riparian states, when a new reality invaded the last quarter of the twentieth century: the exclusive economic zone, also known as the patrimonial sea. Again, the first treaties delimiting the marine and submarine areas—a joint title meant to combine both the economic zone and the continental shelf—were concluded in the Caribbean: on one side between Colombia and its neighbors in the western sector, and on the other between Venezuela and its neighbors in the eastern sector.

Taking into account the recent developments in the Law of the Sea, it is now evident that delimitation of maritime areas under national jurisdiction eventually will be reduced to three categories: territorial seas (12 n.m.); exclusive economic zones or exclusive fishery zones (200 n.m.);[6] and the continental shelf, when it extends beyond the 200-mile limit of the preceding item, or within its current conventional sense for states that have not yet adopted a 200-mile zone, but still feel the necessity of delimiting the shelf beyond the territorial sea—a situation that tends to decline and fade away under the pressure of the economic zone.

The delimitation of internal waters by straight baselines for the purpose of closing them off from the territorial sea will continue to be practiced by riparian states, a right to which the new category of archipelagic states has won formal recognition.

## Principles and methods

Apparently, there does not yet exist a measuring rod good enough to distinguish principle from method in maritime delimitations. Certain publicists, diplomats, and cartographers have applied the term "principle" to categorize equidistant or median lines. However, "equidistance" is but a cartographic method or, at best, a rule for the delimitation of maritime space, but it is definitely not a legal principle. The International Court of Justice in the *North Sea Continental Shelf* cases ruled that the equidistance method cannot be considered a rule of law.[7]

In our view, equity as pursued in distributive justice is the main principle on which maritime delimitations may safely rest, notwithstanding the fact that special circumstances and historic titles may act as corollaries to determine whether the application of the equidistance method would be tantamount, in a given case, to equity. Hodgson suggested with regard to islands that the "solution to the issue raised by [their] effect on equidistance boundaries and seabed allocations may be rationally determined by varying the effects of islands on the limits under specific circumstances. . . . Islands, except in a few specific instances, do not greatly distort territorial sea boundaries due to the narrow limits involved. . . . Inequities become prevalent with increasing distance from the national baselines."[8] Indeed, what makes the median or equidistant line equitable or not is the presence (or absence) and regard (or disregard) for special geographical circumstances such as islands, reefs, shape of the coast (convex or concave), and other particular situations such as the existence or lack of historical title to the waters concerned or to their adjacent seaward extensions, which would rule out the a priori application of a geometric line. Hodgson stressed the fact that "while equidistance is not the sole basis for the delimitation of territorial sea, continental shelf, or seabed boundaries, the principle has been enshrined as a veritable 'conventional wisdom' for maritime limits. It is the only method mentioned in both conventions (territorial sea and continental shelf) and, as a consequence, states find the concept easy to accept due to its proper 'sanctification.'" All this is to be viewed in light of special circumstances or historic rights. Hodgson himself added wisely, "The best boundary between states is one both states accept peacefully."[9]

The methods applied to delimit maritime space have been classified as follows:

(1) Equidistance: by applying a median line every point of which is equidistant from the nearest points on the baselines from which the territorial seas of each of the two states are measured.
(2) Prolongation of final azimuth of land boundary, or prolongation of the general direction of the land boundary.
(3) Line perpendicular to coast at land boundary terminus or to general direction of the coast.
(4) Parallel or meridian of the terminus of land frontier.[10]

On the other hand, several agreements have been reached without reference to any method whatsoever. Such are the agreements between the United Kingdom (Hong Kong) and China (1925), the Anglo-Venezuelan Treaty on the Gulf of Paria (1942), and the Norwegian-Soviet Treaty (1957).[11]

## Straight baselines

A prime factor in the delimitation of offshore areas is the drawing of straight baselines as the basis for the measurement of the territorial sea, where applicable. Three sources are invoked under international law to support a coastal state's right to counterbalance the effect of deep indentations in its coastline or that of a fringe of islands along it and in its immediate vicinity: (1) principles of customary international law as gathered from state practice before any jurisprudence or positive law had been established; (2) the judgment of the International Court of Justice in the *Anglo-Norwegian Fisheries* case; and, (3) the Geneva Convention on the Territorial Sea and the Contiguous Zone. The Geneva Convention will be superseded by the future Caracas Convention, which, however, is not likely to introduce any substantial changes in the above respect. Of the three sources mentioned, the *Anglo-Norwegian Fisheries* case constitutes the link between custom and convention, for, in the words of McDougal and Burke, "in upholding the validity of the baselines claimed by Norway, the Court authorized the inclusion of waters beyond traditional bays and ports within internal waters." [12]

Beside the fact that more than 70 coastal states have availed themselves of this right either according to the words and spirit of the Geneva Convention or according to their own interpretation of that convention, the establishment of such baselines has meant the seaward advancement of the territorial sea belt, irrespective of its specific breadth. The probability of disputes arising has thus been increased, not only because a state may question its neighbor's measures if it considers itself affected but also because new situations of overlapping jurisdictions may arise where they could not possibly have existed before the establishment of straight baselines.

## Development of maritime boundaries

Maritime delimitation started with the territorial sea, took a leap forward with the continental shelf and has come of age with the exclusive economic zone, assuming that no "creeping jurisdiction" will stretch it beyond the limits laid down in the 1980 draft convention.

At the Hague Conference for the Codification of International Law half a century ago, the voice of the maritime powers was the only one that was heard. The United States submitted a proposal that attempted "to view all the problems of delimitation [of the seaward and landward limits of the territorial sea] as a whole, and to set forth a body of rules both simple in application and definite in result." [13] Without going into detail, the important point regarding delimitation that must be singled out from the Hague Conference is the set of guidelines for delimitation, not the specific techniques. In this sense, we must stress the fact that the cartographic methods proposed for the seaward limit of the territorial sea (such as the drawing of arcs of circles instead of straight baselines) were strongly recommended for the purpose of diminishing the waters under national jurisdiction to a minimum.

Two decades later, the International Law Commission, confronted with the task of codifying the Law of the Sea, was "faced with a relative void" in the area of maritime boundaries.[14] Rapporteur François requested a group of experts to evaluate the four methods described for the delimitation of the territorial sea, and their opinion favored the rule of equidistance; they did, however, add the recommendation to negotiate a solution if the median line did not meet the standards of equity.

The 1945 Truman Proclamation on the continental shelf stressed that "boundaries should be determined by the United States and the state concerned in accordance with equitable principles."[15] Equity was invoked in the subsequent proclamations of Saudi Arabia, Iran, the Arab Emirates of the Gulf (now the United Arab Emirates), and Nicaragua.[16]

At the Geneva Conference in 1958 the issue was raised before the two committees that dealt with the territorial sea (and contiguous zone) and the continental shelf, respectively. Article 12 of the Convention on the Territorial Sea and the Contiguous Zone considered both types of cases—i.e., where the coasts of two states are opposite or are adjacent to each other—as it established the median line by forbidding the states concerned, failing agreement to the contrary, to extend their territorial seas beyond such median line. The convention did allow, however, under the same article, that this method could be set aside in cases where it was necessary by reason of historic title or other special circumstances to delimit the territorial sea in a different way. By virtue of Article 24 these provisions apply *mutatis mutandis* to the contiguous zone, save that the exceptions are not valid for contiguous zones.

When it came to the delimitation of submarine areas, Article 6 of the Convention on the Continental Shelf was split into two paragraphs, one dealing with a shelf adjacent to the territories of two or more states whose coasts are opposite each other and the other dealing with a shelf adjacent to the territories of two (only two) adjacent states. In both cases the boundary shall be determined by agreement. In the absence of an agreement, and unless a boundary line is justified by special circumstances, the boundary shall be the median line in the former case and the equidistance line in the latter.[17]

Five years after the latter convention came into force, these provisions underwent their first trial as Denmark and The Netherlands sought to test the opposability of the rule of equidistance to the Federal Republic of Germany, which had not ratified the convention. The argument for opposability rested on the grounds that the convention had won approval *erga omnes* and that no special circumstance could be held to prevail in that part of the North Sea coast of western Europe. The judgment in the *North Sea Continental Shelf* cases was based on three main elements: the application of the equidistance rule among the parties concerned was not compulsory; there was no one single method of compulsory application; and delimitation should be achieved through negotiations according to equitable principles and taking account of all circumstances, allowing to each party the natural prolongation of its territory which does not overlap on the natural prolongation of the territory of its neighbor.

The judgment produced the dual effects of diminishing the dependency on equidistance and pressing for a more fluid formula at the Third United Nations Conference on the Law of the Sea, which was to convene soon. Immediately after the judgment was published, Qatar and Abu Dhabi signed an agreement in which equidistance was but partially and practically honored (20 March 1969); and sometime later Indonesia and Malaysia felt free to negotiate a practical agreement which took into account their special geographical interrelationship (27 October 1969).[18]

On the other hand, as soon as the United Nations decided to examine Malta's proposal and set up the Seabed Committee and then the Third Law of the Sea Conference, it became evident in the light of the *North Sea Continental Shelf* cases that the application of equidistance within the short scope of the territorial sea was still reliable and basically equitable—in the absence of special circumstances or historical titles—but would not be deemed so when dealing with the full scope of the 200-mile economic zone or the entire continental margin. Thus, the Geneva provision was maintained almost intact for the territorial sea (Article 15 of the draft convention) and eliminated for the contiguous zone (which would virtually become an interior belt within the exclusive economic zone). On the other hand, the draft convention deals with the exclusive economic zone and the continental shelf in a similar way as stated in Articles 74 and 83, respectively:

> The delimitation of the exclusive economic zone [the continental shelf] between states with opposite or adjacent coasts shall be effected by agreement in conformity with international law. Such an agreement shall be in accordance with equitable principles, employing the median or equidistance line, where appropriate, and taking account of all circumstances prevailing in the area concerned.[19]

Both articles make room for the settlement of disputes as well as for provisions regarding arrangements of a practical nature pending the negotiation of the final agreement. Agreements already existing between states shall not be affected.

This text deviates from the Geneva provision on shelf delimitation by stressing agreement according to international law as the first recourse, establishing equity as the principle for negotiations, and employing equidistance where appropriate and taking account of all prevailing circumstances. Geneva had recognized equidistance as mandatory in the absence of an agreement and if special circumstances did not justify another delimitation; but not until the International Court of Justice had discerned that states such as Denmark and The Netherlands would benefit from equidistance beyond the bounds of equity did the international community realize that equity as a principle had to be enshrined in the positive law of delimitation. The application of equidistance may be in perfect accordance, or may be at odds, with equity, according to the caprices of geography.

Nevertheless, the debate would resume every time the issue came up before the Second Committee of the conference. It was still identified as a hard-core issue when the Informal Composite Negotiating Text, twice revised (1975–79), turned in 1980 into a "negotiation text" but not a "negotiated text," to quote the late Shirley Hamilton Amerasinghe, president of the conference and of its predecessor, the Seabed Committee.[20] Discussions still focused on whether the criterion should be the equidistance as principle or the principle of equity. A negotiating group under the chairmanship of Judge Eero J. Manner from Finland had not reached a compromise when the conference adjourned in Geneva in 1980. The following is a selective list of states in opposition on this issue.

| Region or subregion | States favoring equidistance | States favoring equity |
|---|---|---|
| Europe | Spain, United Kingdom, Denmark, Yugoslavia, Greece, Malta | Ireland, France, Turkey |
| Africa | Nigeria | Algeria, Libya, Morocco, Madagascar |
| Asia | Japan | Pakistan |
| South America | Chile | Argentina |
| Caribbean Sea | Colombia | Venezuela[21] |

It is easy to spot local maritime boundary disputes behind the respective stands of states hailing from the same region or subregion, irrespective of whether a settlement has been reached: Spain and France, the United Kingdom and Ireland, Greece and Turkey, Malta and Libya, Colombia and Venezuela. The narrow maritime *lebensraum* of a continent such as Europe set on micropeninsulas and adjacent islands suggests that equidistance does not cut through the offshore claims of coastal states as it threatens to do when the effect is projected over wide oceanic space, as is the case of African, Asian, and Latin American countries bordering on the ocean. This general deduction has to allow for particular cases, such as West Germany, which battled against equidistance though it is a riparian of a semienclosed sea. If we had to formulate a hypothesis for the Caribbean, we could suggest that, barring historic titles or special circumstances, the rule of equidistance could provide a sound solution whenever it does not collide with equity. On the other hand, special circumstances will tend to lessen the dependence on equidistance and lead to negotiations inspired by equitable principles. When every delimitation in the Caribbean has been accomplished, there may be a tie between the two tendencies with a slight advantage for equidistance because of the limited geographic scope and the influence of European schools favoring equidistance. At any rate, it must be remembered that, while equity does not rule out equidistance, equidistance may cause inequity.

## The Caribbean mosaic: fundamental facts

One fundamental fact about the Caribbean outlook on maritime problems is the multiplicity of political, economic, social, juridical, and cultural (linguistic) patterns interwoven within its general structure. Whether it is the cause or the consequence of the lack of a coherent concept as to what should be understood by Caribbean identity, or a combination of these, is an issue that falls beyond the scope of this paper.

About thirty-eight political entities are encompassed by the Greater Caribbean—taken here to include the states surrounding the Caribbean Sea and the Gulf of Mexico and including the Bermuda archipelago. These entities include a superpower, the United States, and modest colonies, such as the Cayman Islands; Spanish-speaking, continental communities on the high cordillera and Hindi-speaking, Asian communities on the flat plains of the demerara; the ultramarine departments of the French Republic and the only Marxist-Leninist states in the hemisphere. There is no similar subregion on the globe that can provide as much diversity.

As soon as the economic need for maritime expansion began to be felt

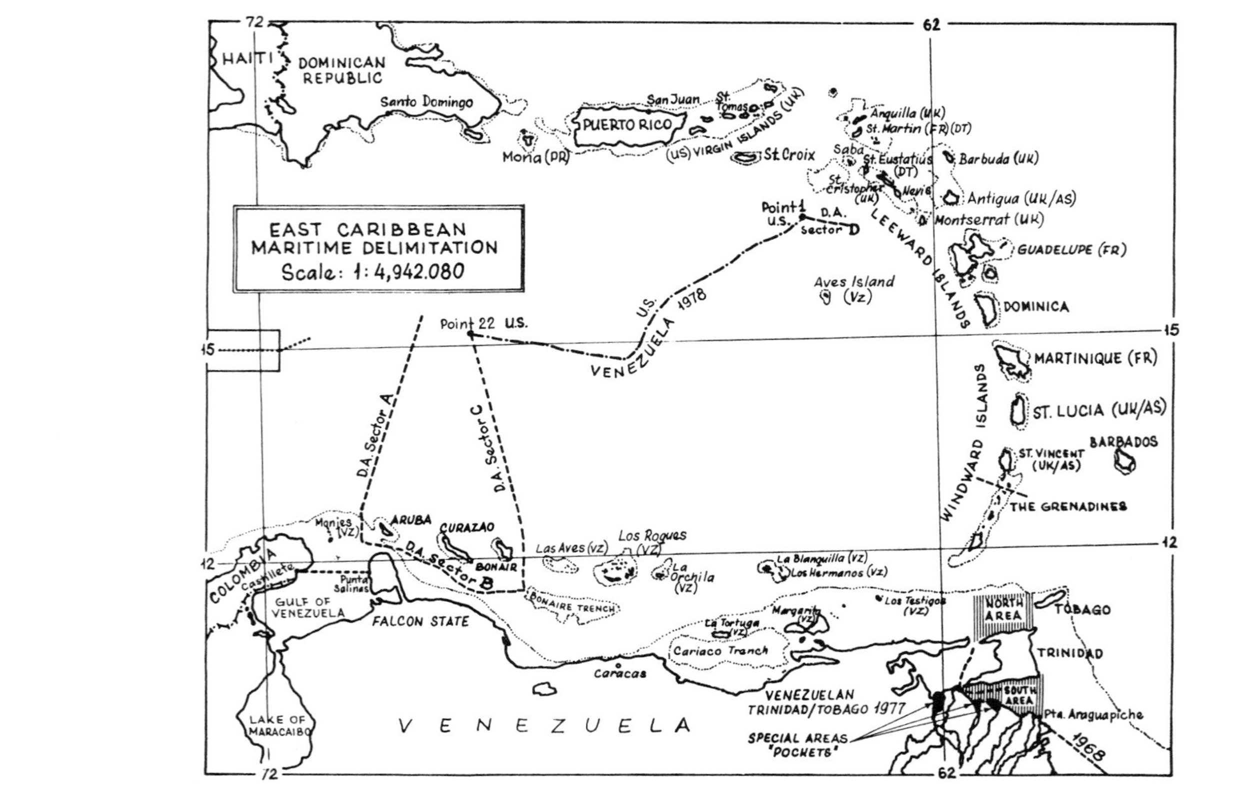
EAST CARIBBEAN
MARITIME DELIMITATION
Scale: 1: 4,942.080
HAITI
DOMINICAN REPUBLIC
Santo Domingo
Mona (PR)
PUERTO RICO
San Juan
St. Tomas
(US) VIRGIN ISLANDS (UK)
St. Croix
Anguilla (UK)
St. Martin (FR) (DT)
Saba
St. Eustatius (DT)
St. Cristopher (UK)
Nevis
Barbuda (UK)
Antigua (UK/AS)
Montserrat (UK)
LEEWARD ISLANDS
GUADELUPE (FR)
DOMINICA
Point 1 U.S.
D.A. Sector D
Aves Island (Vz)
U.S. VENEZUELA 1978
Point 22 U.S.
D.A. Sector A
D.A. Sector C
D.A. Sector B
MARTINIQUE (FR)
ST. LUCIA (UK/AS)
ST. VINCENT (UK/AS)
BARBADOS
WINDWARD ISLANDS
THE GRENADINES
Monjes (VZ)
ARUBA
CURAZAO
BONAIR
Las Aves (VZ)
Los Roques (VZ)
La Orchila (VZ)
La Blanquilla (VZ)
Los Hermanos (VZ)
Los Testigos (VZ)
COLOMBIA
Castillete
Punta Salinas
GULF OF VENEZUELA
FALCON STATE
BONAIRE TRENCH
La Tortuga (VZ)
Margarita (VZ)
Cariaco Tranch
Caracas
NORTH AREA
TOBAGO
TRINIDAD
SOUTH AREA
Pta. Araguapiche
1968
VENEZUELAN TRINIDAD/TOBAGO 1977
SPECIAL AREAS "POCKETS"
LAKE OF MARACAIBO
V E N E Z U E L A
72
62
15
12

after World War II, the Greater Caribbean was the first area in the world to be affected. Even during the short period of Nazi military ascendancy in Europe, Great Britain had set her eyes on the potential oil resources of the Gulf of Paria and had reached an agreement with Venezuela on the division of the submarine areas of that gulf, the first treaty of its kind in the world (Caracas, 26 February 1942). The pattern of annexing the continental shelf to the emerging territory of a colony spread throughout the British imperial system from Trinidad and Tobago, to the Bahamas and Jamaica in 1948, then to British Honduras (Belize) and the Falkland Islands (Islas Malvinas) in 1950, as well as to the Arab Emirates of the Gulf and to Malaysia.[22]

The Truman Proclamation followed the Paria Treaty in 1945, inaugurating a new era in the Law of the Sea as states claimed sovereign rights over the resources of the submerged lands beneath their epicontinental waters. The legal regime of the submarine space enunciated by the United Kingdom (through the Paria Treaty) and the United States (according to the Truman Proclamation) reflected the liberal, Western, Anglo-Saxon legacy: full respect for the principle of the freedom of the seas. There was little that a partner like Venezuela could do then to alter the pattern suggested by Great Britain: "We both share the shelf but do not meddle with the freedom of the high seas beyond our respective territorial limits." That approach continued, however, to fit very neatly within Venezuela's scheme as an oil-exporting country until the seventies, when the value and potential of marine resources had to be reassessed as it became evident that it was possible to reconcile the freedom of navigation and other traditional freedoms of the high seas with state jurisdiction and control over interests such as fisheries, oil, marine research, and environmental protection. Such a reconciliation was suggested by the new trends that seemed to pervade the emerging Law of the Sea through the Maltese proposal (1967), the Santo Domingo and Addis Ababa Declarations (1972 and 1973, respectively) and the Third United Nations Conference.

Nevertheless, it should be borne in mind that, while the postwar trend regarding the continental shelf—whether of the Anglo-Venezuelan or the Truman style—was registered physically in the Greater Caribbean, its philosophy was rooted in the heritage of the liberal, capitalist West. The next move came from those continental Latin American nations who could afford, by both geographic standards and regional prestige, to follow the example of the United States, modifying it to accommodate their legitimate interests. President Avila Camacho of Mexico issued a proclamation in which a claim was made to the epicontinental water of the shelf for the sake of fishery conservation.[23] Several Central American republics echoed the 200-mile "heresy" announced in the shelfless South Pacific by Chile and Peru (1947), to be joined later by Ecuador in the Santiago Declaration of 1952. During the fifties, the Caribbean was not able to respond to the maritime policy of the oceanic South American countries and chose to adhere to the moderate line drawn by the Organization of American States at such meetings as the Tenth Interamerican Conference (Caracas, 1954), the Third Meeting of the Interamerican Jurisconsult Council (Mexico, 1956), and the Specialized Interamerican Conference on the Preservation of Natural Resources, Submarine Shelf, and Seawater (Ciudad Trujillo—now Santo Domingo—1956). The Conference of Ciudad Trujillo virtually ushered into the inter-American community what the International Law Commission was preparing for the Geneva Conference. The so-called Geneva regime was not able to stretch its life for more than one decade, roughly corresponding to the sixties, before it fell under severe questioning. It was also during the sixties that the Latin American countries bordering on the Atlantic Ocean joined hands with their Pacific neighbors and convened the Montevideo Conference for the 200-milers (May 1970) and the Lima Conference for the whole community (August 1970). At Lima, Colombia approved the Declaration of Latin American States on the Law of the Sea. Mexico adopted the position that the extension of jurisdiction could only reach the 12-mile limit. Venezuela voted against the declaration precisely because it took into account the peculiar situation of vital maritime routes in the Caribbean.[24] Nevertheless, the Lima meeting drew the attention of these three Latin American and Caribbean nations to the void in maritime law that had to be filled.

Because of the specific weight of its maritime usefulness, the potential value of the Caribbean as a marine emporium had gone almost unnoticed until the early seventies. Its submarine worth as supplier of oil and gas had been warranted even under the Geneva regime. A compromise formula was thus called for to reconcile these two needs: on the one hand, a narrow sovereign belt (territorial sea) with a consequent open sea for navigation and overflight and, on the other, state control for making rational use of the biological resources. In fact, it was the particular situation of the Caribbean that shaped the legal figure of the patrimonial sea, declared at the Conference of Santo Domingo (9 June 1972) and later rebaptized as the exclusive economic zone.[25]

### *The Geneva regime in the Greater Caribbean*

The Greater Caribbean region more or less accepted the Geneva regime during its brief biological cycle of the sixties. Haiti ranked second in the world in ratifying all the Geneva conventions (29 March 1960). Mexico and Venezuela (with certain reservations) became parties to all four conventions; Colombia chose the resource-oriented conventions and left out the conventions on the high seas and territorial sea. The Dominican Republic became a party to all four. During the early years of their independence, the English-speaking Caribbean countries appeared to favor accession to the Geneva conventions but do not any more: Trinidad and Tobago acceded to the Convention on the Continental Shelf in 1968 and Jamaica to the Fishery Convention in 1964. The republics of the Central American isthmus have been quite reluctant: Guatemala has been party to the Conventions on the High Seas and the Continental Shelf since 1961; Costa Rica accepted the same conventions in 1972. Since the Santo Domingo Conference, not a single accession has been reported.[26]

*Straight baselines*

Some of the Caribbean states have availed themselves of the provisions embodied in the Geneva Convention on the Territorial Sea to draw straight baselines capable of affecting future negotiations on delimitation. The Geographer of the United States Department of State has registered the following:

*Dominican Republic*: By virtue of Decree-Law No. 186, of 6 September 1967, ten sectors on the Dominican coast were closed: four on the north coast and six on the south coast. Two of the bays enclosed: Santo Domingo on the south and Escocesa on the north were declared historic bays.[27]

*Venezuela*: By virtue of Decree No. 1152, of 9 July 1968, a straight baseline was drawn across the delta of the Orinoco River. Since Venezuela claims the Essequibo area, currently under Guyana's control, the decree was meant to establish the baselines for Venezuela's territorial sea in a sector enclosed between the dividing line of the Essequibo River and Punta Araguapiche, the northern tip of the delta. By constructing a straight baseline from the latter to a point situated off the southern tip of the delta, the decree stated that the territorial sea and contiguous zone would be measured from the straight baseline in that sector and from the normal baseline outside that sector to the dividing line of the Essequibo. Article 4 affirms that the "straight baseline at the mouth of the River Essequibo will be in accordance with that of the neighbouring state"[28] (see maps, pp. 28, 35, and 41).

*Haiti*: By virtue of a decree of 6 April 1972, the Republic of Haiti announced the drawing of a series of connecting baselines around the whole extension of its coasts. The Geographer of the U.S. State Department interprets the measure as based on "an implied baseline system" that involves the Haitian half of Hispaniola Island and closes the whole of Gonaive Bay.[29]

*Cuba*: Decree-Law No. 1 of 24 February 1977 struck a series of 124 baselines all around the island starting from Cape San Antonio in the northwest and proceeding clockwise through the southeastern extreme of Punta Maisí and thence back to the starting point passing in front of the United States naval base of Guantanamo. The Cuban system encloses minor and major bays (Nipe, Guacanayabo, and Batabano, between the main island and Isla de Juventud), as well as all the fringes of the islands parallel to the coastline (Jardines de la Reina).[30]

## Cartographic representation of maritime borders

Before discussing delimitation agreements already concluded in the Caribbean it may be necessary to recall that not all lines shown on maps as dividing maritime space represent true demarcations. Such lines may only be cartographic devices to simplify the description of land areas involved, as was stressed by Boggs.[31] This would be the same cartographic device, quite common in Caribbean maps, employed to separate island jurisdictions visually, such as across Mona Passage, between Guadeloupe and Dominica, or between Guadeloupe and Antigua.[32]

The definition to be bestowed on the line running along meridian 82° West, which separates the jurisdictions of Nicaragua and (insular) Colombia, may not be clear, since the source was not a delimitation treaty applicable to specific claims *strictu sensu* (Bárcenas Meneses–Esguerra Treaty of 24 March 1928) but a diplomatic note attached to the ratification instruments when exchanged by Irías Gil and Esguerra in 1930. The note stated that the Archipelago of San Andres and Providence (recognized as belonging to Colombia in conformity with said treaty) “does not extend westwards from longitude 82° West.”[33]

## Establishment of economic or fishery zones

As soon as the 200-mile limit, for the exclusive economic zone or for the fishery conservation zone, proved to have won the debate over the emerging Law of the Sea, the Greater Caribbean again became the area of major delimitation concentration. Since the mid-seventies, its two main halves, the Gulf of Mexico and the Caribbean proper, have vied for the first round of successful negotiations.

The Gulf of Mexico has been the easier and more accessible of the two. The United States and Mexico had no difficulty in extending the 12-mile limit established by their treaty of 23 November 1970 for the clarification of the Rio

Grande boundary and the creation of maritime boundaries in the Pacific Ocean and the Gulf of Mexico. By exchange of notes on 24 November 1976, these points were provisionally extended to the outer end of the 200-mile limit, both across the Gulf of Mexico and into the Pacific Ocean. On 4 May 1978, the Maritime Boundary Treaty between Mexico and the United States, signed in Mexico City, declared the aforesaid lines definite.[34] This treaty was not passed by the Senate.

On 26 July 1976, Mexico and Cuba succeeded in delimiting their exclusive economic zones. The area involved covers the Yucatan Channel and part of the Yucatan Basin.[35]

Most states bordering on the Greater Caribbean have also unilaterally established either a fishery zone (United States in 1976 and Guyana in May 1977) or an exclusive economic zone, more or less in agreement with the Informal Composite Negotiating Text: Costa Rica (May 1975), Mexico and Guatemala (June 1976), Cuba (January 1977), Dominican Republic (February 1977), Haiti (April 1977), Bahamas (June 1977), Suriname (April 1978), Venezuela and Colombia (July 1978), Nicaragua (December 1979), and Honduras (1980).[36]

## A complex model: the Colombian-Venezuelan case

In the Caribbean proper, it is safe to suggest that most of the delimitations already negotiated have been directed at influencing the unsuccessful fifteen-year dialogue between Colombia and Venezuela regarding the northwestern corner of the Gulf of Venezuela. One of the most difficult issues to arise in this field, the so-called *differendum*, combines characteristics that are not confined to the maritime and juridical aspects of the delimitation. A historical process that dates from the separation of Venezuela and New Granada in 1830 has marked the Colombian-Venezuelan controversy, endowing it with distinct features: *geographic*, involving the double situation of potential delimitation between adjacent and opposite coasts simultaneously, plus the existence of a special circumstance, the Venezuelan archipelago of Los Monjes (The Monks) off the continental coast of Colombia; *geologic*, as it is presumed, but not yet proven, that the seabed of the gulf may conceal considerable wealth in oil and natural gas; *biologic*, as it is reputed for its shrimping grounds and demersal species; *naval and maritime*, as all sea-lanes leading to oil-rich Lake Maracaibo pass through the gulf; *historical*, because Venezuela has always exercised full sovereignty over the waters of the gulf in conformity with international law; *political*, since Venezuela and Colombia are friendly neighbors, partners within the Andean subregional pact, and democratically governed; *sociological*, because oil-rich Venezuela absorbs a great deal of Colombia's social problems through illegal immigration and labor competition; and *psychological*, because, despite friendship and goodwill, Venezuela has been the historical loser in land frontier disputes with her neighbor, resulting in the shrinking of her western provinces and, most ironically, in the definite loss in 1922 of the province of Guajira Peninsula, a loss which converted Colombia into a riparian of the Gulf of Venezuela and thus a potential claimant of maritime titles therein.[37]

Such complex circumstances are not easy to combine in one single case. The crux of the problem is that Colombia has been quite fortunate during the century-old controversy that shifted the land boundary where it met the sea, from Cabo de la Vela, terminus of the Spanish Captaincy-General of Venezuela, to various points retreating eastward and thence southward to where it now stands at the village of Castilletes, 23 miles within the perimeter of the gulf on its northwestern shore.[38] An arbitration award pronounced by the Spanish Court in 1891 declared that the boundary started in Los Frailes, a place never found by the Demarcation Bilateral Commission. The commission, nevertheless, adopted Castilletes in 1900 as the starting point for the boundary without any legal grounds whatsoever. Due to its weak internal situation Venezuela did not impugn the commission's execution of the award but tried to obtain compensations along the common land border. Venezuela succeeded in conserving for itself the coast of the gulf through mutual concessions until a new difference arose regarding the interpretation of the award and another arbitration was agreed upon. In 1922, the Swiss Federal Council confirmed the location of the land border in Castilletes, not because it had revised the Spanish award but because it considered terminated the work of the Demarcation Commission. In 1941, the two parties signed a Demarcation and Fluvial Navigation Treaty, in which they solemnly declared that all their boundary differences had been settled once and for all.

A few years later, Whittemore Boggs was approached in Washington by a Colombian attaché who wanted to be shown "how to lay down a 'boundary' between Colombia and Venezuela in these waters. . . . Perhaps no more interesting problem of this sort could have been posed, for the example has about all possible variations."[39]

Professor Boggs, practicing with a pair of dividers on a map which was printed within the context of one of his famous articles, has borne the responsibility for the hardship that both countries have since experienced. An excel-

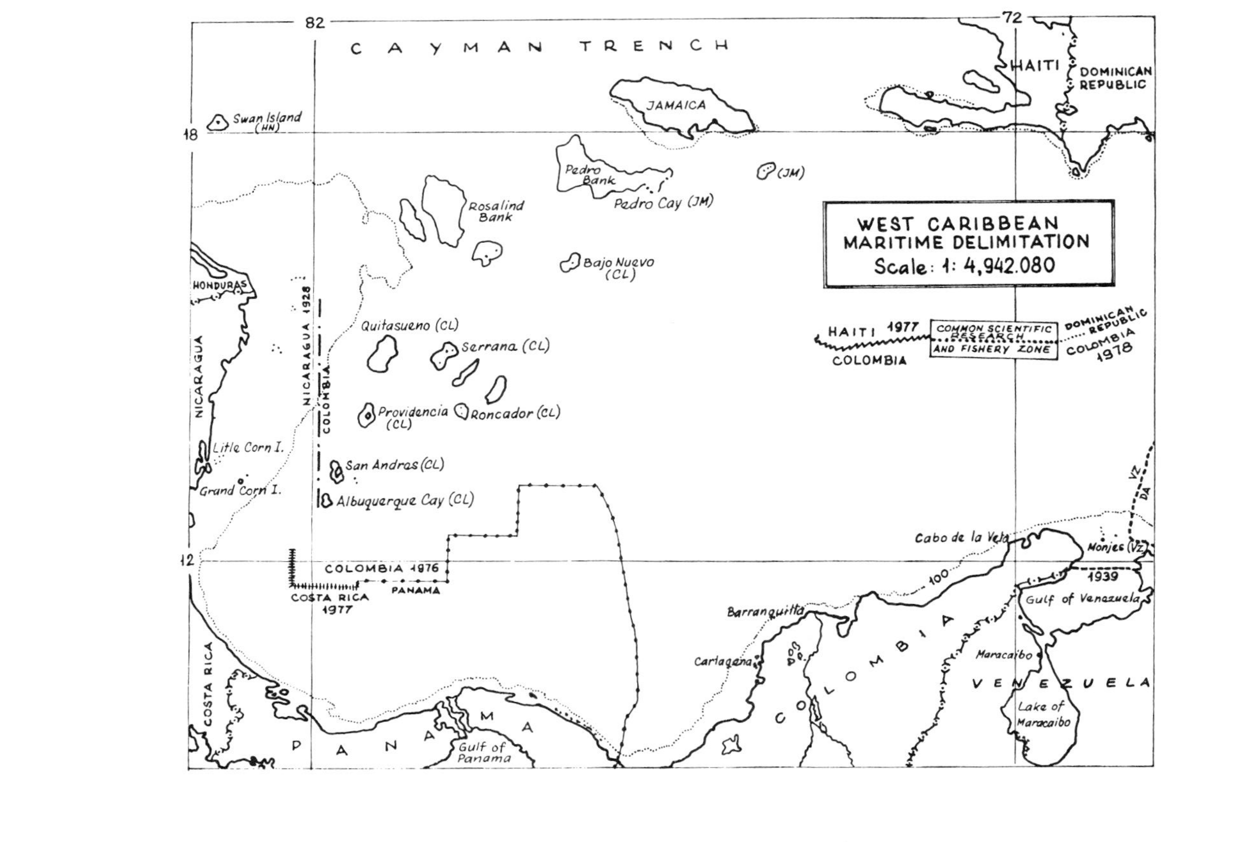
WEST CARIBBEAN
MARITIME DELIMITATION
Scale: 1: 4,942.080
CAYMAN TRENCH
82
72
18
12
HAITI
DOMINICAN REPUBLIC
JAMAICA
Swan Island (HN)
Pedro Bank
Pedro Cay (JM)
(JM)
Rosalind Bank
Bajo Nuevo (CL)
HONDURAS
NICARAGUA
NICARAGUA 1928
COLOMBIA
Quitasueno (CL)
Serrana (CL)
Providencia (CL)
Roncador (CL)
Litle Corn I.
Grand Corn I.
San Andras (CL)
Albuquerque Cay (CL)
HAITI 1977
COLOMBIA
COMMON SCIENTIFIC RESEARCH AND FISHERY ZONE
DOMINICAN REPUBLIC
COLOMBIA 1978
COLOMBIA 1976
PANAMA
COSTA RICA 1977
COSTA RICA
PANAMA
Gulf of Panama
Cabo de la Vela
Monjes (VZ)
VZ
DA
100
1939
Gulf of Venezuela
Barranquilla
Cartagena
COLOMBIA
Maracaibo
VENEZUELA
Lake of Maracaibo

lent specialist in this field, Boggs had no idea of the 110 years of bitter controversy over the land frontier which had just been buried. By acting on the latter-day arrival of Colombia to a 23-mile strip of coastline within the northwestern corner of a historic Venezuelan gulf as if it constituted an original fact and an untouchable datum, he stirred up fresh desires in Colombia which Venezuela, in the light of the historic process, considered inadmissible and potentially aggressive. Since the coast where the land boundary hits the gulf at Castilletes is concave, Boggs's median line pierced the closing baseline between Castilletes and Punta Salinas. Venezuela had fallen back on this line in 1939, while negotiating the Demarcation Treaty with Colombia, precisely to afford room for the latter's claim to the coastal strip on the gulf, as per arbitration awards which had to be complied with. After the outbreak of World War II, Venezuela closed her bays by a decree (16 September 1939) which was cited in the pleadings in the *Anglo-Norwegian Fisheries* case.[40] In 1940, Venezuela protested the incursion of the French warship *Barfleur*, which attacked two Italian merchant vessels, *Alabama* and *Dentice,* within the gulf and reiterated in diplomatic correspondence with the French minister its pronouncement on the historic character of the waters of the gulf.[41] Boggs even ignored the right of the Venezuelan Monjes archipelago to generate maritime jurisdiction although he acknowledged that the islands belonged to Venezuela.[42]

Colombia's diplomats and policy-makers have stuck to Boggs's map for thirty years, claiming it is the only acceptable solution. The American expert has won fame and praise for his exercise. In 1964, Colombia parceled out land and submarine territory with the intention of granting oil concessions, before any approach to Venezuela had been registered. That started initial conversations and three subsequent stages of formal negotiations that may be summarized as follows:

PHASE 1: 1970–73

Colombia: (ratified Convention on Continental Shelf)

Proposed: Delimitation along the Median Line (known as Boggs's) and nonrecognition of Monjes's rights to maritime jurisdiction.

Venezuela: (ratified all four conventions, reserving delimitation provisions)

Proposed: The closure of the gulf south of the parallel through Castilletes, and the land frontier to be projected across the gulf following its general direction.

Result: Deadlock.

PHASE 2: 1975–77

Proposed: The Boggs median lines are indirectly incorporated into a plan which would have allowed for joint exploitation in the disputed sectors in which the above claims overlapped.

Result: Rejection by Venezuelan opposition parties.

PHASE 3: 1979–80

Proposed: The Gulf would be jointly closed from the Monks toward the peninsular coasts of both countries, and its maritime space partitioned as internal waters. Venezuela would conserve sovereignty over the sector south of the 1939 closing line; Colombia would acquire similar rights over one-seventh of the gulf's extension. The line would be carried northward toward the central axis of the Caribbean, thus delimiting respective economic zones.

Result: Defeat of the project by Venezuelan public opinion. President Herrera Campins announced official rejection on 12 March 1981.[43]

It is clear that the problem is much more deep-rooted than one generated solely by a potential maritime delimitation. The historic background and psychological implications, which Professor Boggs did not consider, add considerably to its complexity. Thus, a popular movement was founded in Venezuela with the aim of proving that the 1891 Spanish award established Colombia's right over 23 miles of gulf coastline but not over the Gulf's waters, thus declaring Colombia's boundary a "dry shore" (*costa seca*). Two lawyers and two retired colonels have filed lawsuits before Venezuela's Supreme Court of Justice demanding the annulment of the 1941 treaty. The fact that these movements have been able to stir public opinion against a hasty agreement caught the Venezuelan government by surprise, leading President Herrera Campins to hand over the draft treaty to the press with the promise not to sign it if there was no consensus—a consensus which has been conspicuously absent.

### The perimetric delimitations by Colombia and Venezuela

The government of Colombia devised an aggressive strategy to promote its maritime claims in the Gulf of Venezuela. While trying to achieve the best out of Phase 2 as described, Colombia decided to resolve other delimitations off her Pacific and Caribbean coasts as quickly as possible, in order to secure the pragmatic objective of gaining acceptance for equidistance lines as bases of maritime delimitation and spreading the impression that, while everybody else was an understanding neighbor and easy to get along with, Venezuela was not.

Before adopting her own law on the 200-mile economic zone, Colombia succeeded in delimiting "marine and submarine areas" with Ecuador in the open Pacific (by following the parallel of the terminus of the land frontier) in August 1975. The pattern was soon introduced into the Caribbean area through a treaty with Panama, signed on 20 November 1976. The treaty with Costa Rica which followed on 17 March 1977 was exclusively applicable to a sector within the Caribbean Sea. Colombia finally negotiated two more treaties, one with the Dominican Republic on 13 January 1978 and the other with Haiti in March of the same year.[44]

Elsewhere I have commented on these developments: "Strictly speaking, only two of the Colombian treaties can be quoted as mainly based on the median line. This was achieved in the respective treaties with the Dominican Republic and Haiti, where there are no special circumstances whatsoever, and where the coasts are safely opposite and apart. In the Panama-Colombia treaty, lip service is paid to the median line. It is barely applied to a series of six successive points in the Caribbean and in the Pacific, only to be dismissed for all practical purposes, as both countries struck vertical and horizontal lines off the little islands and cays that Colombia possesses in the Caribbean, on the Central American continental shelf. The rest of the Pacific boundary was drawn on latitude 5° N, parallel to the already-fixed boundaries among the South Pacific nations and accepted by Colombia herself in her treaty with Ecuador. Colombia's treaty with Costa Rica does not follow any median line."[45]

These efforts were not lost upon the Venezuelan government, which launched its own policy for delimiting maritime boundaries in the eastern Caribbean. Venezuela faced a different situation though, because of (a) the proximity of some of her insular neighbors and the existence of corollary problems such as oil-prospecting, fishing, or potentially overlapping sovereign rights; (b) the extracontinental seat of the treaty-making power for the Dutch, French, or British territories in light of the Law of the Sea Transitional Provision; and (c) the case of Aves (Birds) Island, a tiny stretch of sand and purslane in the vicinity of the Leewards which is part of Venezuelan territory (recognized by the arbitration award of 1865) and a potential source of friction in light of Article 121 of the ICNT which limits the maritime jurisdiction of uninhabited rocks, or rocks unable to sustain economic life of their own, to the territorial sea and the contiguous zone.[46]

President Andres Perez's administration (1974–79) arrived at a favorable solution for a series of fishing incidents in the Gulf of Paria by signing an agreement with Trinidad and Tobago on 12 December 1977. Nothing in the new agreement interferes with standing maritime delimitations or introduces new boundaries; in fact, no reference was made to the 1942 treaty on the division of the seabed. Two fishing areas were designated to the north and to the south of Trinidad, respectively, in which both parties are allowed to fish, except within two miles from their coasts. Within the southern area, three special pockets have been designated in Venezuelan internal waters to which artisanal Trinidadian fishermen will be admitted but not trawlers.

During the last week of March 1978, Venezuelan diplomacy achieved the signature of two treaties: one, with the United States of America on 28 March during President Carter's visit to Caracas; the other, in Wilhelmstadt, capital of the Netherlands Antilles, during President Andres Perez's visit to these islands. Negotiated separately, each treaty was in perfect agreement with the particular situation of the other parties concerned. In both, Venezuela won full recognition to the maritime jurisdiction of Aves (Birds) Island, with the favorable result of confirming her jurisdiction over 80,000 sq. km. of economic waters that would have probably constituted a disputed issue with several interested parties. By acknowledging Venezuela's rights without demur, two naval and maritime powers such as the United States and The Netherlands paved the way for other governments concerned in the Eastern Caribbean to follow suit.

Nevertheless, there are basic differences between these treaties. Because the United States does not recognize any maritime claims that have not yet been sanctioned in a comprehensive universal convention on the Law of the Sea (though it exercises fishery conservation jurisdiction within a 200-mile limit), the introduction to the bilateral treaty with Venezuela is quite brief: the need to establish precise and equitable maritime limits. The geodesic lines between 22 points on a continuous maritime border are embodied in Article 2, joining the ends on both inner sides where the Venezuelan–Dutch Antilles line is interrupted. (The Netherlands Antilles are composed of two sectors, quite wide apart, in between which Venezuela faces Puerto Rico and the Virgin Islands.) Without naming the maritime areas thus delimited, the parties renounce sovereign rights or jurisdictional claims over the waters, the seabed, and the subsoil thereof on the opposite side of the border. This treaty came into force on 24 November 1980.[47]

The treaty with the Netherlands Antilles, whose prime minister signed it on behalf of the Queen of The Netherlands, is much more comprehensive and far reaching. Besides the fact that it succeeds in drawing a boundary over two main sectors (the Major Antilles: Curaçao, Aruba, and Bonaire off the Venezuelan mainland; the Minor Antilles: Saba, St. Eustache, and half of St. Maarten) separated by a space in which the line between Venezuela and the United States had to fit, the treaty establishes a *modus operandi* for transit passage between the Major Antilles and the Venezuelan mainland and regulates other activities such as marine pollution, common geological beds, conservation and exploitation of living resources, and scientific research.

The Venezuelan–Dutch Antilles boundary is not based on the median line, but that fact did not prevent its application in some segments between opposite coasts when it was accepted by both parties. On the lateral border of the Antilles zone, the actual boundary favored Venezuela slightly, on the assumption that continental masses engender more jurisdiction proportionally than do smaller islands. The Antilles were compensated by a potentially oil-rich corner. The treaty came into force on 15 December 1978.[48]

On 3 March 1979, Venezuela negotiated its third boundary agreement with the Dominican Republic. With both coasts quite apart and opposite, the median line was applied along a considerable part of the boundary extension with the explicit mention that the basis taken for this agreement would not constitute a precedent for the Dominican Republic's delimitation with third parties (Article 7). A common regime for marine pollution control, scientific research, and conservation of resources was included.[49]

Following the coming to power of the Christian Socialist government in Caracas, the delimitation policy was resumed and a new agreement was negotiated with France regarding maritime jurisdictions west of its ultramarine insular territories of Guadeloupe and Martinique. Negotiations on the maritime boundary with Trinidad and Tobago were also activated. The treaty with France, signed on 17 July 1980, runs along meridian 62°48′50″ and does not seem either to follow any known formula or to satisfy Venezuelan public opinion, though it was warmly welcomed in Paris.[50] [The agreement was nonetheless discussed and approved by the Venezuelan Congress in 1982.—Ed.]

Thus, the Colombian-Venezuelan dispute over the border across a sector of the Gulf of Venezuela has triggered ten different agreements without producing its own solution. Colombia has been keen on denominating her treaties as "Delimitation of Marine and Submarine Areas and Maritime Cooperation" in order to link the issue of the economic zone, which requires an amplification of the strict delimitation by the addition of clauses on marine pollution, scientific research, and resource conservation, to that of the gulf. Venezuelan public opinion has watched this process closely lest it be unduly "petrolized" and converted into a mutual relationship or cooperation over waters regarded

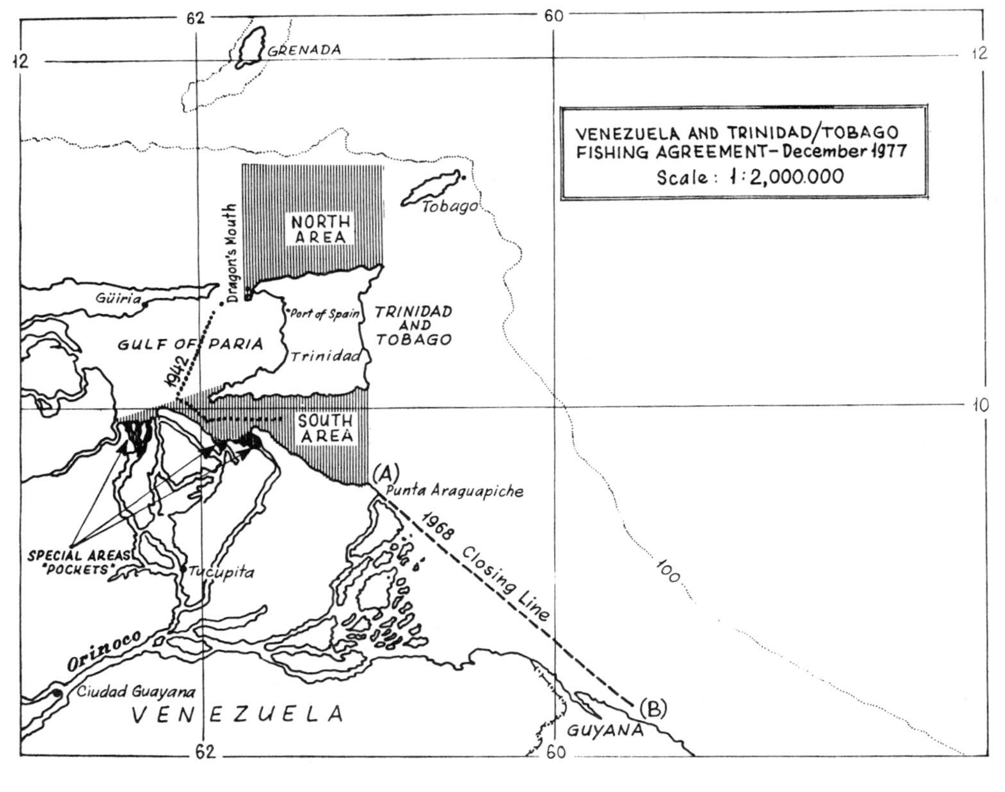
VENEZUELA AND TRINIDAD/TOBAGO
FISHING AGREEMENT – December 1977
Scale: 1:2,000.000
GRENADA
Tobago
NORTH AREA
SOUTH AREA
Dragon's Mouth
Güiria
Port of Spain
TRINIDAD AND TOBAGO
GULF OF PARIA
Trinidad
1942
(A)
Punta Araguapiche
1968 Closing Line
(B)
100
SPECIAL AREAS "POCKETS"
Tucupita
Orinoco
Ciudad Guayana
VENEZUELA
GUYANA
62
60
12
10

by Venezuela as historic and internal. Indeed, the Venezuelan treaty with the Dutch Antilles recognizes the vital and historic importance to Venezuela of the Gulf of Venezuela, the complex of fundamental interests that characterize it, as well as the maritime transit to and from Venezuela.

The perimetric delimitations by Colombia in the western Caribbean and by Venezuela in the eastern sector have been very rewarding on their own merits. Apparently, the precautions taken by each party to defend its thesis on maritime delimitation (equidistance versus equity) meant little when geopolitical pressure, late in 1980, counseled both countries to try to liquidate their controversy through the hasty and unconstitutional draft treaty of October 1980. It was immediately rejected by Venezuelan public opinion, with a vehemence never attached before in any country of the region to such technical and juridical problems as those embodied in a potential maritime delimitation.[51]

## The geopolitical pressure of delimitation

Because of multiple interests at variance, neighboring states do not necessarily share the same views on the importance, need, or urgency of maritime delimitation. Two states are lucky if they share a mutual interest in identifying a potentially delimitable area and a similar degree of urgency in negotiating an agreement. Under such circumstances negotiations become meaningful and do not usually introduce other pending political issues. In fact, one barometer of political maturity of a state is the framework within which it operates its maritime policy. The rule: the less a government politicizes its maritime or marine policies, the more mature and serious it is.

On the other hand, apathy in delimiting maritime space can only denote either lack of material interests at stake or extreme administrative indigency. Nonetheless, as soon as some particular motivation arises (oil prospecting, danger from a pollution source based in a neighboring country, a fishery joint venture, etc.), the void is likely to be quickly filled. The very nature of development drives toward the direction of diminishing indifference.

The most common type of case in the Caribbean is one that may be labeled lopsided or unilateral interest: one party is anxious to fix its maritime limits, but its neighbor is not. In such cases, the next step depends on the degree of the so-called lopsided interest, for as long as there is no real economic urge, states usually wait for the right moment. When internal pressure on the interested state is high, it feels obliged to politicize the question in one of two ways: (a) by adjusting the original and preferred position it would have adopted in the first round of negotiations by offering its neighbor a package deal that might include concessions, either in terms of sharing the benefits of the common area, or in other fields in which the neighbor may be interested (trade, communications, scientific cooperation, transfer of technology, oil supply, etc.); or (b) by forcing negotiations by granting or announcing the imminent granting of oil concessions or fishing licenses beyond the potential boundary, or by defying the maritime sovereignty of the other state in a way that induces it to come to the negotiating table, as, for instance, when the demandant state attempts fishing in its neighbor's waters on the ground that the limits are uncertain, ambiguous, or unilateral.

From a political point of view, maritime boundary disputes are usually critical. When there are no vital interests at stake, states tend to ignore the issue; when they do acknowledge the matter it is most certain that a specific interest or motivating factor has caused the change of attitude through a "critical" evaluation of what is at stake.

The specific issues or motivating factors that turn a normally dormant state of affairs into a lively one do not possess equal weight. Prospecting for oil and gas is the unchallenged leader, followed at a respectful distance by fishing. Control of marine pollution and environmental rationality lag behind as a poor third, but their position will definitely improve when ocean policy managers find out how interrelated marine pollution and fishery conservation actually are. Environmental concern will acquire a different dimension when the Caribbean gets its own version of a *Torrey Canyon* or an *Amoco Cadiz*.[52]

So far, the three ranges of interest have been easy to detect in the Greater Caribbean:

| | |
|---|---|
| *Mutual interest:* | Gulf of Mexico, United States–Mexico–Cuba |
| *Mutual lack of interest:* | Caribbean proper, most of the recently independent ministates, usually of European heritage |
| *Lopsided interest:* | Continental countries versus insular domains; also between states of distinct juridical legacies unable to get together in the absence of a common, specific interest |

## Patterns of delimitation problems in the Caribbean

Concurrent and diverse realities convert the Greater Caribbean into one of the most complex areas for maritime delimitation. In fact, as mentioned, there is no other area in the world that exhibits a comparable diversity of factors and interests. The 90-odd delimitation agreements that remain to be concluded eventually may stumble upon one or more of the following problems.

*Where the process involves concurrent consideration of unsettled disputes concerning sovereignty over continental or insular territory.*—Even when a land boundary dispute is deemed settled—at a high cost and not quite conclusively as in the case of the Colombian-Venezuelan controversy—the development of a maritime boundary dispute based on a shaky settlement is bound to mix up both.

A concurrent unsettled land boundary dispute hangs over the potential maritime delimitation between Venezuela and Guyana. The former claims the whole Essequibo territory, which means that it cannot negotiate with Guyana any maritime delimitation unless there is previous agreement on the terminus where the land boundary hits the sea. Venezuela's decree already mentioned was considered a provocation by the government of Guyana, while Venezuela was only applying international legal dispositions on what it considered to be national territory.

Another case exists between Guatemala and Belize. As long as the Central American republic considers the former British colony as part of its territory and fails to recognize its independence, there is no way to draw maritime limits.

The United States will not be able to delimit marine areas off Puerto Rico with the Dominican Republic as long as the latter sustains its claim to Mona Island.

Haiti cannot delimit the shallow waters of Albatross and Grappler Banks with Jamaica before the status of Navassa Island is settled. Navassa is considered a U.S. unincorporated territory and houses a U.S. lighthouse.

One of the major potential conflicts in the area is the dispute between Nicaragua and Colombia over San Andres and Providencia Archipelago. It does not only stand in the way of delimiting the economic zones of the states involved but may lead to a wider conflict that may extend beyond the maritime rights of the parties concerned and spread to the fragile geopolitical chessboard of Central America.

*Where political tensions preclude delimitations, whether there is an unsettled territorial dispute not involving maritime jurisdiction or where relations are severed or truly bad.*—Relations between neighbors may become extremely tense when conflictive issues are taken seriously. A territorial dispute that does not involve maritime jurisdiction may aggravate relations and preclude fresh negotiations as each party accuses the other of being stubborn. This is the case in the territorial dispute between Guyana and Suriname over the upper basin of the Corentyne.

Following the New Jewel Movement that took power in Grenada in 1979, relations with Trinidad and Tobago have deteriorated, and under such circumstances states may allow time to pass. Cuba has no special predilection for the government of Haiti; neither has the Dominican Republic been able to forget a long history of frustrations over the common land boundary.

*Where the states concerned have been deliberately lukewarm or apathetic to the concept of the economic zone.*—This situation is peculiar: it maintains its specific significance for states whose zones would be eventually locked between the zones of their neighbors. Jamaica, for instance, has been an early opponent of the patrimonial sea, advocating instead a "matrimonial sea." Trinidad and Tobago supported the concept at the beginning but has had second thoughts. Such states are not expected to be among the pioneers of delimitation.[53]

*Where the treaty-making power resides in European metropolises which have not taken any initiative to delimit among themselves the economic zones of their dependencies, though they have been willing to do so when a local power has raised the matter.*—Venezuela had no major problems delimiting with the United States, The Netherlands, or France, but it is unlikely that extra-Caribbean powers, attentive to the Transitional Provision and conscious of their decreasing role in the area, will volunteer to do the job for those who are most concerned. Due to the relatively large number of colonial, departmental, or associated entities in the insular Caribbean, not to mention Belize and the French Department of Cayenne, numerous possible delimitations will remain to be undertaken for many years to come. All the Leeward Islands, except Dominica, fall in this category; so do the Cayman Islands, which engender a wide economic area south of Cuba, and the Turks and Caicos, which have to seek with Haiti and the Dominican Republic a point of triple convergence besides their limits with the Bahamas.

*Where the governments concerned have been traditionally land-oriented and hardly interested in marine management.*—This subjective handicap may carry some weight as long as traditional values prevail. Such a relationship with the sea is typical of the Central American isthmus, which formed first under Spanish rule and subsequently through independence and the traditional concepts of agricultural economics that developed on the Central Cordillera. Where attention was paid to the seas, it was to the Pacific, the only exceptions being English-speaking Belize and coastal Honduras (San Pedro de Sula). Although the Central American republics were among the first subgroups to affirm claims to the continental shelf (Declaration of Antigua, Guatemala, 1955), few concrete steps have been taken in the direction of exploring marine resources by their own nationals. After its revolution in 1979, Nicaragua has proclaimed such a policy with the advice and technical help of Cuba. [By late 1981, no maritime delimitation agreements had been registered in Central America.—Ed.]

*Where independence has been recent with not enough time to lay down a modern marine policy.*—This normal stage has to be surpassed as soon as more urgent problems are solved. Dominica, independent since 1979, was devastated by a hurricane. St. Vincent has been reported to be examining its maritime interests. [St. Lucia, on the other hand, signed an agreement with France in 1982.—Ed.]

The evident conclusion is that five ingredients are needed to accelerate the delimitation process in the Caribbean: solution of land-boundary controversies; passage of time and acquisition of experience; decolonization; continuation of the process and the consciousness that every new agreement is a step ahead; and adherence of all schools of political action and cultures to the delimitation process.

## Settlement of disputes

Part of the issue of maritime delimitation is the legal procedure to be adopted for the settlement of disputes, as well as the interim measures states may take pending a final settlement. From a political point of view, however, the effectiveness of a multilateral treaty as a source of positive international law should not be deduced from the provision or lack of mechanism for dispute settlement. The more value that states attach to the issues to be submitted to compulsory dispute settlement, the less they seem to favor their incorporation into the treaty, unless, of course, they possess the political power to influence the legal procedure. Within the Geneva system, the two innovating conventions took two different stands on dispute settlement. The Fishery Convention included an elaborate mechanism under Article 9, which has never been invoked; the Continental Shelf Convention contained no such mechanism, yet various states have not hesitated to resort to all channels in order to protect their vital interests. Greece's endeavor to bring Turkey to the International Court of Justice, though unfruitful, is an example that proves how hard a state will pursue compulsory settlement when it believes its interests are served—not only economic but political as well—taking into account that any negotiated settlement may be interpreted by public opinion of either side as an excessive territorial concession.

Nevertheless, an objective observer is tempted to agree with the French delegate De Lacharrière when he said that there had to be a strong link between the establishment of maritime jurisdictions, their delimitation, and procedures for the settlement of disputes. As the Third Law of the Sea Conference introduced the concept of the economic zone into positive law, he added, it ran the risk of fostering endless controversies among countries that will become neighbors through the creation of the exclusive economic zone.[54]

What the Law of the Sea Conference has been trying to do is to achieve a compromise solution. The future Convention on the Law of the Sea opens various channels to ensure the settlement of disputes likely to develop from the multiple uses of the ocean and its resources. Its substantive contribution is embodied in Part XV (Settlement of Disputes), to which various annexes are tied: Annex V (Conciliation), Annex VI (Statute of the Law of the Sea Tribunal), Annex VII (Arbitration), and Annex VIII (Special Arbitration Procedure).

Article 15 on the delimitation of the territorial sea has not been linked to any specific provision on the settlement of disputes, except inasmuch as any other article of the convention potentially might be. Articles 74 and 83, however, do require the states concerned (a) if no agreement can be reached within a reasonable period of time, to "resort to the procedures provided for in Part XV," and (b), pending an agreement, to "make every effort to enter into provisional arrangements of a practical nature . . . without prejudice to the final delimitation."[55]

Part XV requires an exhaustive perusal that falls beyond the limits of this paper. The main points we consider relevant can be summarized by comparing the titles of the articles that compose Section 1: obligation to settle disputes by peaceful means; obligation to exchange views; obligations under general, regional, or special agreements; procedure when dispute is not settled by means chosen by the parties; and conciliation.

Section 2 of Part XV is dedicated to the compulsory means for the settlement of disputes relating to the interpretation or application of the convention, among which—and subject to the provisions of section 3 *ut infra*—the parties shall be free to choose, according to article 287, among the Law of the Sea Tribunal constituted in accordance with Annex VI; the International Court of Justice; an arbitral tribunal constituted in accordance with Annex VII; a special arbitral tribunal constituted in accordance with Annex VIII for one or more of the categories of disputes specified therein (fisheries, protection and preservation of the marine environment, marine scientific research, and navigation, including pollution from vessels).

Section 3, which provides the guidelines for the particular categories of disputes, lists under Article 297 the categories to which Section 2 is applicable. Article 298, Optional Exceptions, identifies the categories of disputes for whose settlement a state may declare, upon expressing its consent to be bound by the convention, that it does not accept any one or more of the procedures specified in Section 2 without prejudice to the obligation arising under Section 1 (general obligations and conciliation). The first of three categories thus indicated is that "concerning the interpretation or application of articles 15, 74, and 83 relating to sea boundary delimitations, or [that] involving historic bays or titles."

Nevertheless, this optional exception is not absolute. Article 298 requires that states making such a declaration "shall" accept conciliation of the dispute at the request of any party to the dispute if negotiations between the parties do not lead to an agreement within "a reasonable period of time." From such submissions, the same text has expressly excluded "any dispute that necessarily involves the concurrent consideration of any unsettled dispute concerning sovereignty or other rights over continental or insular land territory."

Subparagraph (ii) states that "after the Conciliation Commission has presented its report, which shall state the reasons on which it is based, the parties shall negotiate an agreement on the basis of that report; if these negotiations do not result in an agreement, the parties shall [may], by mutual consent, submit the question to one of the procedures provided for in section 2 of Part XV, unless the parties otherwise agree."

As may be observed, the exact wording of numeral (ii) makes the whole difference. While the Informal Composite Negotiating Text (Revision 2) employed the auxiliary verb "shall"—mandatory—the new text proposed by Negotiating Group 7, embodied in the Draft Treaty, substitutes "may." It is unlikely that states will reverse the latest version, especially if one analyzes, politically, the composition of the delegations that reject a compulsory settlement. A state may, of course, withdraw its formal declaration, or choose voluntarily any one of the procedures provided for under Article 287. The actual compromise, if it stands, goes a little beyond traditional conciliation and stops before the threshold of compulsory jurisdiction.

## A regional alternative for settlement of disputes

The question of a regional alternative for settling disputes elicits two kinds of replies: legal and political. From the former point of view, the developing Law of the Sea not only encourages regional and subregional cooperation but also provides the framework and the incentives for them.[56] Article 282 of Part XV addresses the issue:

> If States Parties which are parties to a dispute relating to the interpretation or application of this Convention have accepted, through a general, regional or special agreement or some other instrument or instruments, an obligation to settle such dispute by resort to a final and binding procedure, such dispute shall, at the request of any party to the dispute, be referred to such procedure. In this case any other procedure provided in this Part shall not apply, unless the parties to the dispute otherwise agree.

According to numeral (iii) of subparagraph (a), paragraph 1, Article 298, "any dispute which is to be settled in accordance with a bilateral or multilateral agreement binding upon those parties" is always released from the procedure which may be described as "necessary conciliation and subsequent contingent compulsory settlement," contained in Article 298.

Furthermore, Article 311 which appears for the first time in the Draft Convention, allows two or more states to negotiate agreements, applicable to their mutual relations, by virtue of which they may only modify or suspend the application of those provisions of the convention which are not incompatible with the achievement of its goals and the application of the basic principles announced therein and provided that the provisions of such agreements do not affect the rights and duties of the remaining parties to the convention. Thus the states bordering the Greater Caribbean may establish their own regional alternatives for settlement of disputes, not only those that ensue from differences on boundaries but also those which reflect other sources of friction. In doing so, however, they can neither transgress the basic principles announced in the convention nor, because of the rule *res inter alios acta*, aspire to make opposable their norms and decisions to third parties.

The legal frame is set by the convention itself; any region or bloc—whether bound by a common geographical contour or by the same legal school of thought—may, before the convention comes into force, adopt its own procedure or set of procedures and act according to the explicit provision of Article 282.

It remains to be seen whether such a move is politically viable and convenient. To begin with, the convention has all but covered every probable procedure and means, so that, from a technical and juridical point of view, there are almost no alternatives to those the convention offers. What a regional, subregional, or juridico-cultural community of states might do is to conclude an agreement that singles out and chooses that particular means or procedure of dispute settlement which accords with its tradition and style, notwithstanding the fact that the Law of the Sea Tribunal and the Special Arbitral Tribunal constitute a new legal "adventure" for everybody and require, besides jurisprudence and experience in international law, a sound basis in marine science and technology.

We may well pose the following questions: Is there any real need for a regional approach to dispute settlement? Is there any real possibility of creating a regional subsystem?

Both questions will in the end elicit negative replies but not without a positive by-product. Without prejudging the possibility of enhancing regional cooperation under Article 311, paragraph c, there does not seem to exist a real need for a regional approach to the settlement of disputes on maritime boundaries, either in the Caribbean or anywhere else in the world. This is because the questions involved are technical and geographical, usually very specific and self-contained, and not prone to acquire regional, subregional, or continental characteristics. The maritime boundary between two given states is like a marriage relationship between any two people: there is always a certain amount of specificity in each relationship and there is a universal institution called marriage, but there cannot be a regional version of this unique universal institution from which every couple of subscribers draws an individual experience. As it is argued that there are distinct cultural customs of matrimony, the same argument may be carried to our subject as we add that the variety of legal and judicial systems may be taken as a basis for the selection of the most convenient means or procedure to be applied in conformity with the cultural mosaic of the Caribbean. This should be read in light of the two principal legal systems of the area: Anglo-Saxon common law and the Napoleonic codes of Latin America. When talking law, it is easier for the English-speaking peoples of the Caribbean to understand one another than to understand Latin Americans, and vice versa. The Dutch-speaking communities share such affinities with the Anglo-Saxons, the French-speaking communities with the Latins. Bowing before these elemental facts, it may be advisable for CARICOM nations to decide on a practical procedure that meets the needs of their judicial, political, and linguistic cultures and apply it wherever possible to settle controversies that do not concern third parties. About twenty potential delimitations are pending among states and states-to-be in the English-speaking and Dutch-speaking Caribbean alone. Indeed, the delimitation of maritime areas around the Leeward Islands may be discussed in a roundtable conference and prepared as a package. Once CARICOM nations decide that it is time to do the job, they will be readily convinced that their common political, judicial, and cultural heritages warrant a family-affair choice of the best means to settle any future disputes within the context of the Law of the Sea. The English-speaking communities of the Caribbean are not only bound by this heritage but are fortunate enough to command access to the sources of a common jurisprudence which they share with formerly British Africa, as well as communication with the essence of the philosophy of the ancient laws of Asia, both Hindu and Moslem.

As for the Spanish-speaking Latin Americans, it will be more difficult for them to avail themselves of their common cultural, judicial, and political heritage because a century and a half of individual independence is time enough to emphasize individual differences. Economic development of unequal magnitudes has added its burden. There is no doubt that it was the Latin American legal unity that shaped the Law of the Sea to the interest of developing nations since the early fifties, making it possible to bequeath to the world the notion and concept of the patrimonial sea or the exclusive economic zone. But once it comes to decisions on national sovereignty, each state will act on its own vital interests which, in this particular field, may be exactly the opposite to those of its neighbor: Colombia and Venezuela, Chile and Argentina, Peru and Ecuador, Colombia and Nicaragua, to mention just the ones in the news. What all Latin American nations agree upon, undoubtedly, is the need to settle disputes by peaceful means, as prescribed in the Charter of the United Nations and in the Charter of the Organization of American States, in strict conformity with the principles of their cultural heritage and the practice of civilized nations.

## Conclusion

Since the Santo Domingo Conference on the Patrimonial Sea, the countries that border the Greater Caribbean have not met again to discuss their maritime problems. True as it may be that delimitation principles, methods, and rules, as well as procedures and means of dispute settlement, are universal as a philosophy and bilateral as a praxis—thus excluding an intermediate regional approach—this is not the case with maritime problems arising from navigation, fishing, conservation of natural resources, protection of the marine environment, control of pollution, and transfer of marine technology. All these activities, even if they are carried out in other maritime regions of the world, are definitely influenced by the geographic setting of the area concerned, its marine biology and chemistry, its hydrography and oceanography, and its ecological realities. They are also influenced by the specific social, economic, political, and legal circumstances that govern maritime and naval relations and generate problems such as oil slicks that invade tranquil tourist beaches, tuna that are caught by outside vessels (legally or not), trawlers that clean off shrimping grounds on one side and cause disaster on the other, wastes that are dumped into the sea from land-based industrial societies, and the menace of radioactive pollution. Such activities—the ones that constitute the exploitation of the resources of the sea and the use of its surface for communications—are the ones that warrant a regional outlook. In these circumstances there is no excuse for the Caribbean nations not to act on a regional basis.

If there is one semienclosed sea in the world that fully warrants a regional outlook on its maritime and marine problems, it is the Greater Caribbean. In this sense, it becomes the archetype of regional cooperation. So far, the Food and Agriculture Organization's (FAO) West Central Atlantic Fishery Commission (WECAF) and the International Oceanographic Commission's (IOC) IOCARIBE have been doing an excellent job, each in its particular field and often jointly. The workshop they cosponsored with the United Nations Environment Program (UNEP) on Marine Pollution in the Caribbean and Adjacent Regions, held in Port of Spain in 1976, is an exact example of what is needed and of what needs to be continued, amplified, and institutionalized. The call for a coordinated fishery program in the area is not more or less urgent than the call for a regional convention on the control of marine pollution, on the lines of the 1976 Barcelona Convention for the Mediterranean.

Meanwhile, the process of maritime delimitation cannot be reversed. Once set into motion, it has to be carried farther, as soon as possible, to the last remaining corner. The reason and the philosophy behind it should never be the reduction of this bountiful sea into maritime fiefdoms of riparian nations, each closed on itself in an anachronistic version of the Middle Ages, but its preparation toward regional cooperation and mutual assistance on the basis that the Caribbean is one common square, like Venice in its days of glory, open to all who live by its shores and are ready to work in order to enjoy the best of its bounties under the sway of a new law, based on the ecological principle of the rational use of natural resources and on the legal principles of equity and international social justice.

## Notes

1. During the past 12 years, the geographer of the U.S. Department of State has published about 90 cases in the series LIMITS IN THE SEAS. These cases include straight baselines and the delimitation of territorial seas, continental shelves, fishing zones, and economic zones.

2. *Id.*, no. 36, at 221 (3d rev. 1975).

3. *Id.* at 104.

4. *Id.* at 160.

5. ROBERT D. HODGSON AND ROBERT W. SMITH, *Boundaries of the Economic Zone*, in LAW OF THE SEA: CONFERENCE OUTCOMES AND PROBLEMS OF IMPLEMENTATION 183–206 (Miles and Gamble eds. 1977). For an analysis of the Paria Treaty, *see* KALDONE NWEIHED, *Venezuela's Contribution to the Contemporary Law of the Sea*, 11 SAN DIEGO L. REV. 603–33 (1974).

6. Writing in the sixties, Lewis Alexander observed that "some countries have [fishing] zones which are delimited from the same baseline as the territorial sea, and extend three, six, nine, or more miles seaward of the territorial limits. For other countries, the fisheries zones are not only greater in breadth than the territorial sea but measured from different baselines, generally straight baselines, which themselves may be considerably seaward of the low water line from which the territorial zone is measured": *Offshore Claims of the World*, in LAW OF THE SEA: OFFSHORE BOUNDARIES AND ZONES 71–84 (Alexander ed. 1967).

7. [1969] I.C.J. 3 at 36, para. 56; 45, para. 82.

8. ROBERT D. HODGSON, *Islands: Normal and Special Circumstances*, in LAW OF THE SEA: THE EMERGING REGIME OF THE OCEANS 137–99 (Gamble and Pontecorvo eds. 1973).

9. *Id.*

10. HODGSON AND SMITH, *supra* note 5, at 185; and Separate Opinion of Judge Ammoun, [1969] I.C.J. at 100.

11. *See* Separate Opinion of Judge Ammoun, [1969] I.C.J. at 127, para. 26.

12. MYRES S. MCDOUGAL AND WILLIAM T. BURKE, THE PUBLIC ORDER OF THE OCEANS 120 (1962).

13. S. WHITTEMORE BOGGS, *Delimitation of the Territorial Sea: The Method of Delimitation Proposed by the Delegation of the United States at the Hague Conference for the Codification of International Law*, 24 AM. J. INT'L L. 541–55 (1930).

14. HODGSON AND SMITH, *supra* note 5, at 184.

15. Proclamation No. 2667, 13 BULLETIN, Dept. of State, 485 (1945); reproduced in 4 DIGEST OF INTERNATIONAL LAW 756–57 (prepared by M. Whiteman 1965).

16. Separate Opinion of Judge Ammoun, [1969] I.C.J. at 127, para. 26.

17. 15 U.S.T. 471 at 474 (1964–1); 499 U.N.T.S. 311 at 316 (1964).

18. The Geographer, U.S. Dept. of State, *supra* note 1, Ser. A, no. 1, at 1–2 (1970).

19. DRAFT CONVENTION ON THE LAW OF THE SEA (INFORMAL TEXT), UN DOCS. A/Conf.62/WP.10/Rev. 3 and A/Conf .62/WP.10/Rev. 3/Corr. 1, reproduced in 19 INT'L LEGAL MATERIALS 1129, at 1171 and 1174 (1980).

20. Explanatory Memorandum by the President of the Conference, UN Doc. A/Conf.62/WP.10/Rev.3, Add. 1, reproduced in 19 INT'L LEGAL MATERIALS 1129, at 1130, para. 9 (1980).

21. UNCLOS III, press release, 2 September 1980.

22. ZDENEK J. SLOUKA, INTERNATIONAL CUSTOM AND THE CONTINENTAL SHELF 71–74 (1968).

23. UN Legislative Series, UN Doc. ST/LEG/Ser. B/1, at 13.

24. DERECHO DEL MAR, OAS Doc. Ser. Q. II. 4 CJI-7,v. 1, at 249–64.

25. *See* 2 KALDONE G. NWEIHED, LA VIGENCIA DEL MAR 495–527 (1974).

26. Multilateral Treaties in Respect of Which the Secretary-General Performs Depositary Functions, UN Doc. ST/LEG/Ser.D/13, 565–88 (1980).

27. The Geographer, U.S. Dept. of State, *supra* note 1, Ser. A, no. 5, at 1 (1970).

28. *Id.*, no. 21, at 1 (1970); and GACETA OFICIAL DE LA REPUBLICA DE VENEZUELA, no. 28, at 672 (1968).

29. The Geographer, U.S. Dept. of State, *supra* note 1, no. 51 (1973).

30. *Id.*, no. 76, at 1–4 (1977).

31. S. WHITTEMORE BOGGS, *Delimitation of Seaward Areas under National Jurisdiction*, 45 AM. J. INT'L L. 240–66, at 240 n.2 (1951).

32. *See* for example PHILIPS'S MODERN SCHOOL ATLAS 91 (1958).

33. CARLOS ALFONSO AYALA JIMENEZ, EL CARIBE: MAR INTERIOR DE LAS AMERICAS 127 (1978).

34. The Geographer, U.S. Dept. of State, *supra* note 1, no. 45 (1972).

35. JORGE A. VARGAS, TERMINOLOGIA SOBRE DERECHO DEL MAR 101–4 (1979).

36. J. F. PULVENIS, *La Mer des Caribes*, 84 REVUE GENERALE DE DROIT INTERNATIONAL PUBLIC 310–27 (1980).

37. MARY JEANNE REID MARTZ, *Delimitation of Marine and Submarine Areas: The Gulf of Venezuela*, 9 LAWYER OF THE AMERICAS 301–17 (1977). *See also* KALDONE G. NWEIHED, LA DELIMITACIÓN MARITIMA AL NOROESTE DEL GOLFO DE VENEZUELA (1975).

38. In his famous letter written in Kingston, Jamaica, in 1815 and addressed to his friend Mr. Henry Cullen, the liberator Simón Bolívar thought that New Granada (later Colombia) and Venezuela might form one single state, for which he recommended a new capital (Las Casas) be built at Bahiahonda (30 km. to the east of Cabo de la Vela), "in the boundary of both nations." SIMON BOLIVAR, CARTA DE JAMAICA 126 (1972).

39. BOGGS, *supra* note 31, at 262 n.35.

40. 3 *Anglo-Norwegian Fisheries Case*, I.C.J. PLEADINGS 344 (1951), and 4 *id.* at 195. *See also* MAURICE BOURQUIN, *Les Baies Historiques*, in MELANGES GEORGE SAUSER-HALL 41 (1952).

41. LIBRO AMARILLO DE LOS ESTADOS UNIDOS DE VENEZUELA 423, 430 (1941).

42. BOGGS, *supra* note 31, at 261.

43. ANIBAL R. MARTINEZ, LA DIFERENCIA CON COLOMBIA (1981); KALDONE G. NWEIHED, PANAROMA Y CRITICA DEL DIFERENDO: EL GOLFO DE VENEZUELA ANTE EL DERECHO DEL MAR (1981).

44. AYALA JIMENEZ, *supra* note 33, at 1–61.

45. KALDONE G. NWEIHED, *"EZ" (Uneasy) Delimitation in the Semi-Enclosed*

*Caribbean Sea: Recent Agreements Between Venezuela and Her Neighbors*, 8 OCEAN DEV. & INT'L L. 1–33 (1980).

46. *See* WILLIAM LANE HARRIS, THE AVES ISLAND CLAIMS: A STUDY OF CLAIMS TECHNIQUES (thesis, Vanderbilt University, 1963).

47. GACETA OFICIAL DE LA REPUBLICA DE VENEZUELA, no. 2240, *Extraordinario*, 21 July 1978.

48. *Id.*, no. 2291, *Extraordinario*, 26 July 1978.

49. *Id.*, no. 1634, *Extraordinario*, 28 July 1980.

50. *El Universal* (Caracas), 18 July 1980, at 4, 17.

51. Kaldone G. Nweihed, *Colision Entre la Hipotesis y la Constitucion Colombiana, id.*, 19 January 1981, at A-4.

52. The most serious recent incident was the collision between the tankers *Atlantic Empress* and *Aegean Captain* off Tobago in July 1979. Thirty-six mariners were reported missing, and thousands of barrels of crude oil were spilled into the ocean. For an exhaustive review of vessel-borne pollution, *see* R. MICHAEL M'GONIGLE AND MARK W. ZACKER, POLLUTION, POLITICS AND INTERNATIONAL LAW: TANKERS AT SEA (1979).

53. On the Jamaican idea of a matrimonial sea, "in which there is a community of property among the partners," as distinct from a patrimonial sea, *see* K. O. RATTRAY, A. KIRTON, AND P. ROBINSON, *The Effect of the Existing Law of the Sea on the Development of the Caribbean Region and the Gulf of Mexico*, in PACEM IN MARIBUS: CARIBBEAN STUDY AND DIALOGUE 251–75 (E. Borgese ed. 1974); and LENNOX F. BALLAH, *Applicability of the Archipelago and Mare Clausum Concepts to the Caribbean Sea, id.* at 276–304.

54. 11 UNCLOS OR, Summary Record of Meetings, 8th sess., plen. mtgs., 112th mtg. 12 para. 33 (1980).

55. DRAFT CONVENTION ON THE LAW OF THE SEA, *supra* note 19, at 1171, 1174.

56. J. D. KINGHAM AND D. M. MCRAE, *Competent International Organizations and the Law of the Sea*, 3 MARINE POLICY 106–32 (1979).

# Comments

## *F. V. García-Amador*

THOUGH I am a "Caribeño" myself, I must admit that I am not thoroughly familiar with the regional law of the sea problems. I am therefore grateful to Professors Lewis and Nweihed for all I have learned from their excellent papers.

One of the important aspects of Professor Lewis's paper, in a sense perhaps the most important one, relates to the proposed extensions of the national maritime jurisdictions and their impacts upon the fishing interests of some of the so-called zone-locked or geographically disadvantaged countries of the Caribbean. I would like to raise the question of whether the complaint they make is fully warranted in light of the current position of the Third UN Conference on the Law of the Sea with regard to the nature and scope of said extensions of jurisdiction.

Among the complaints cited in Professor Lewis's paper is, for example, that encompassed in the remarks of the late Sir Eric Williams in 1975 in Caracas: The "extensions of 200-mile fishing or exclusive economic zones would be catastrophic for Caribbean countries that are in a state of virtual dependency on access to fisheries resources of the West and Central Atlantic region."

As Professor Lewis points out, Jamaica's "constant concern was with her status as a zone-locked state." This category of countries—also called "geographically disadvantaged" states—was characterized by the Jamaican delegate in the UN Conference as "those states which were adversely affected in their economies by the establishment of economic zones or patrimonial seas; or states which have short coast lines and could not extend uniformly their national jurisdictions."

If such is the rationale of the complaint, what does this group of Caribbean countries claim? According to the statements made by some representatives, Trinidad and Tobago claimed "preferential rights of access to exclusive economic zones and zones of national jurisdiction"; Jamaica was also prepared to accept 200-mile extensions of exclusive jurisdiction provided such rights of access were recognized.

Undoubtedly, both the complaint and the claim of these and other Anglo-Caribbean countries are fully justified in light of the 1972 Santo Domingo Declaration, and probably it was mainly this declaration that gave rise to their position. Also in light of earlier developments in the Law of the Sea Conference, so far as the Santo Domingo Declaration is concerned, there is no doubt that it reflected the traditional position of Latin American countries in former declarations, beginning with the 1952 Declaration of Santiago followed by those of Montevideo and Lima. All of these declarations ignore entirely the interests of other states.

They ignore as well the interests of the land-locked countries of Latin America, Bolivia and Paraguay, which face problems similar to those of the Anglo-Caribbean countries. Curiously, despite the fact that the Santo Domingo Declaration in its preamble expressly recognizes the peculiar condition of the Caribbean countries and their requirement, accordingly, of special treatment, the text of the declaration does not mention the peculiar situation of these countries of the Caribbean. In many parts of that declaration, however, there are expressions such as "The breadth of this zone [the patrimonial sea] should be the subject of an international agreement, preferably of a worldwide scope." In the paragraph dealing with the high seas, there is the idea of preference for regulation of worldwide scope and general acceptance. In other words, the Santo Domingo Declaration, despite the fact that it came out of a regional conference, is a declaration of worldwide scope, globalist or universalist in its approach.

I wish to mention the position taken by the Inter-American Juridical Committee in its Declaration on the Law of the Sea. In its declaration the committee recognizes that the land-locked states of the region will be authorized, within the zone extending from 12 to 200 miles from the coast, to exploit the living resources within said zone, thereby recognizing their preferential rights vis-à-vis the other states. In this connection, Professor Galindo Pohl—a member of the committee in those days—once said that this is an implicit recognition of the "special interests" of the American land-locked countries. It is a pity that the committee at that moment did not extend this expression to include the zone-locked countries of the region, since the situations are similar.

That is the situation with regard to the Santo Domingo and the other Latin American declarations. In closing I would like to consider the present situation and what we can say about the latest developments in the UN Law of the Sea Conference. Since 1974 some rights have been recognized, and in the draft convention of 1980, Article 70 deals with the rights of states with special geographical characteristics. It is a long article, but the pertinent part reads: "States with special geographical characteristics shall have the *right to participate* on an equitable basis in the exploitation of an appropriate part of the *surplus* of the living resources of the exclusive economic zones of those states of the same region taking into account relevant economic and geographical circumstances of all the states concerned. . . ." The word "surplus" is an important limitation to the right that was not there in the text of 1978. And the right to participate that is in the 1980 UN text does not go as far as the preferential fishing right recognized in the declaration of the Inter-American Juridical Committee.

Now at least there is the recognition of a right that is preferential one way or the other vis-à-vis the rights of other states not belonging to the category of those with which we are now concerned. I mentioned Article 70 to show that there is reason to be optimistic. In this respect, what is important is the beginning; no matter how weakly, the right is recognized. Nothing had happened in the law of the sea in the generation or two before the 1955 Rome Conference, where, by one vote, and for the first time at the international level, there was recognition of the "special interest" of the coastal state in the conservation of the living resources of the high seas. That was the beginning of the process that, through the International Law Commission and the first two UN Law of the Sea Conferences, resulted in the institution of the 200-mile zone. So let us be optimistic about this first step on the part of the Third UN Law of the Sea Conference in favor of the recognition of special rights in favor of the zone-locked, geographically disadvantaged countries.

# Comments

## *Lewis M. Alexander*

I MUST cover my flanks with the normal statement that the views I express are my own and do not necessarily represent those of the United States government. I did not realize that Professor Nweihed would present so much detail on the equidistance-equity principles argument, but I feel in the interests of equity that he should be countered somewhat by those arguments that hold the equidistance line to be not entirely inappropriate. I have two statements to make on this matter.

First, the draft convention says that the delimitation between states shall be effected by agreement in accordance with international law, utilizing the median or equidistance line "where appropriate." Just as the idea that "equity" is a state of mind, so also "where appropriate" is a state of mind.

Second, I believe it was the Venezuelans who pressed the United States for an equidistance line between uninhabited Aves Island and Puerto Rico. In that case they thought equidistance seemed to be the proper line. Also, I think equidistance was proposed for the boundary with the Dutch islands of the Lesser Antilles. It is hard to say which is right and which is wrong. In our negotiations with the Canadians on Georges Bank, it is the Canadians who are pushing for equidistance and the Americans who are in favor of special principles; yet in our other three maritime boundaries with Canada it is the United States which wants the equidistance line and Canada the equitable principles. Equity lies in the eye of the beholder.

Professor Nweihed points out correctly the dichotomy of the maritime boundaries in the Caribbean because, while the Caribbean is a unique area with unique problems, there are certain principles of maritime boundary limitation that are universal. And the Caribbean states are going to have to apply these universal principles while paying attention to local geographical differences.

Perhaps in the Caribbean the potential for joint action is stronger than in other areas of the world, but, looking at the Caribbean as these two speakers have done, I do not see a great deal of evidence that separate countries are giving up investment in favor of joint-venture projects. One way around this problem is the use of joint development zones, such as that between Japan and South Korea which, unable to settle their boundary delimitations, set up such an arrangement. But this has been a rare happening between countries until now.

What are the principles of maritime boundary delimitation? Any lawyer, geographer, or other professional can argue about this definition. I think there are four sources of data on delimitation procedures: global conventions—the Geneva Conventions and the soon-to-be adopted (we hope) Draft Convention, which set out certain terms; various judicial decisions, particularly those of the World Court, including the *North Sea* cases and the *Anglo-French Arbitration* award; state practice, where, I am sorry to say, few compendiums have been made (our office is trying to set up a complete series of state practices so that at least we can draw upon what other people have done); and, finally, negotiation between the parties leading to an agreement. But, as Professor Nweihed points out, how can a nonconsenting adult be forced into an agreement made by its neighbor if it does not want to agree with it?

One statement in Nweihed's paper intrigued and bothered me a little: "One barometer of political maturity of a state is the framework within which it operates its maritime policy. The rule: The less a government politicizes its maritime or marine policies, the more mature and serious it is." I would argue that the Soviet Union politicizes its maritime policy a great deal; does that mean it is not mature and not serious? I think it is very serious. I have discovered that when people come up with generalities like this, their own country usually comes out looking well. There is a theory developed many years ago by a geographer at Yale, the late Ellsworth Huntington, who worked out what he claimed were the most ideal climates of the world. He did a great deal of work, using current scientific reasoning, on what the best and worst climates were, and he ended up with an ideal climate that was very much like that in New Haven, Connecticut!

I was interested in the various states of maritime boundary delimitation noted. First, a "mature" state, judging by the statement I just read, may decide in the abstract that it should settle once and for all its maritime boundaries with its neighbors before incidents arise. I cannot think of very many "mature" states in the Caribbean which decide, before they even see the problem, to delimit their maritime boundaries.

Second, a situation may occur or may be anticipated that prompts a state to begin active negotiations with one or more of its neighbors concerning settlement before a serious problem arises. This has happened in a few cases, for example, the settlement between the United Kingdom and Venezuela in the Gulf of Paria in 1942 well before there was knowledge of oil resources in the area.

A state and its neighbor may both be anxious to settle but may find that no agreement is possible. What do they do? They may decide to go to the Court, but very few have done so. There may be a long-standing boundary dispute that goes on for years and even decades with no settlement and with the states trying to keep incidents to a minimum. The United States has 36 maritime boundaries with its neighbors to settle—36 separate boundaries, including those in the Caribbean and the Pacific as well as those with its immediate continental neighbors. Only *one* of these 36 has been settled with an agreement actually in effect—our boundary with Venezuela. We have more or less an agreement with the Soviet Union between Alaska and Siberia, although this is not a boundary in the technical sense but an 1867 Convention line which stated that all lands found to the east of this line belong to the United States and to the west of it belong to Russia. The status of this boundary itself is still a matter of dispute.

I have two relevant questions that may be rhetorical. What are the pressures on the Caribbean states forcing them to resolve their maritime boundaries? If they have no disputes, particularly in the Lesser Antilles and other areas without definite boundaries, why should they rush to judgment? Obviously they have not done so; either they think it is not important or they have not figured out the mechanism for settling. The map shows many cases of former French and British colonial territories across the water from one another, and the addition of some Dutch territories makes a complicated pattern. The United States is in no great hurry to settle all of its maritime boundaries. We are starting to settle some in the Pacific, mostly in the interest of the tuna industry, particularly between American Samoa and the areas around it. We are also starting to settle boundaries in the Caribbean; for example, we are talking with the British about the boundary between the American Virgin Islands and the British Virgin Islands.

The other question is legal: Once a country achieves independence, what is the status of a maritime boundary negotiated for it as a dependent territory by a metropolitan power? Is the country committed to a decision made while it was a colony? The Trinidad-Venezuelan situation comes to mind, but there are others. We will probably have to have an International Court decision on treaty validity once the country has become independent. That decision may depend upon the conditions under which the country achieved its independence.

# The Caribbean and the Emerging Law of the Sea

*Lennox F. Ballah*

THE LATE prime minister of Trinidad and Tobago, Eric Williams, convinced of the overwhelming disaster facing the majority of Caribbean States in respect of the pending new international agreements on the Law of the Sea, called on these states to seek common approaches to protect themselves against what he perceived as an "impending catastrophe."[1] He proposed on 15 June 1975 that the Caribbean Committee (CDCC) of the Economic Commission for Latin America (ECLA) be convened and that its agenda give "the highest priority to the question of a common Caribbean position on the law of the sea aimed specifically at securing international recognition for a special regime for the Caribbean multigovernmental archipelago."[2] As envisaged, such a regime would, in modification for the Caribbean only of the 200-mile exclusive economic zone, give all Caribbean states and governments equal rights and access to the entire Caribbean Sea with reservation regarding (a) the rights of an individual state to its territorial waters and continental shelf and (b) the freedom of navigation for all states outside territorial waters.

The proposal for a special equitable regime for the Caribbean is analogous to the *mare clausum* concept for the Caribbean Sea, which was put forward in Barbados in November 1971 by the Government of Trinidad and Tobago for discussion at a ministerial meeting of the Caribbean Free Trade Association (CARIFTA) countries on the Law of the Sea. Under this concept,[3] the Caribbean Sea is seen as the heritage of the peoples of the territories that lie in or border it. Title to the resources of the sea vests in all the peoples of the region, with all states having equal access to these resources. The concept is philosophical in nature, and unlike Eric Williams's proposal, is not specific or detailed in scope.

The proposal as outlined bears some similarity to the matrimonial sea concept, propounded by the Government of Jamaica at the specialized conference of Caribbean countries on the problems of the sea held in Santo Domingo on 9 June 1972.[4] That concept, as put forward, would allow coastal states a 12-mile territorial sea in the Caribbean, leaving the resources, both living and nonliving, of the rest of the Caribbean beyond the 12-mile territorial sea limit to be shared equally by the states lying in or bordering the sea. Laudable as the matrimonial sea concept was, it was no more than a pipe dream and stood no chance whatsoever of acceptance at Santo Domingo. The continental mainland countries were not prepared to give up rights to their continental shelves in exchange for access to the largely unproductive waters and narrow shelves of the insular archipelagic Caribbean. In short, to use one concrete example, Jamaica had no "quo" to exchange for Nicaragua's or Colombia's "quid." The rationale for the Jamaican proposal was based on traditional rights of access and on the certain knowledge of the inequitable distribution of the resources of the Caribbean Sea, the major portion of which clung to the continental mainland. Prime Minister Williams saw those geographical inequities seriously compounded by the emerging Law of the Sea concept of the 200-mile exclusive economic zone (EEZ). That concept was in fact emerging in 1975 when he spoke of it as one of the threats to the insular Caribbean community. Today, though not yet formally adopted in a Third United Nations Convention on the Law of the Sea, the regime of the 200-mile exclusive economic zone can properly be said to be developing progressively into a rule of law.[5] Insular Caribbean territories as well as those other states, disadvantaged geographically by the adoption of EEZs, have had little or no success in their efforts to reverse this emerging trend at the Third United Nations Conference on the Law of the Sea (UNCLOS III). It is in light of these developments that I seek to examine the emerging Law of the Sea as it affects the Caribbean.

The term "Caribbean" as used here is restricted to the Caribbean multigovernmental archipelago or the insular Caribbean territories stretching from the Republic of Cuba in the northwest through the Greater and Lesser Antilles to Barbados and Trinidad and Tobago in the southeast. The reference to the "emerging Law of the Sea" is a reference to the negotiating texts that have come from the various sessions of UNCLOS III, the most recent of which available at the time of publication is the Draft Convention on the Law of the Sea (informal text).[6] I will attempt to show that the emerging Law of the Sea will confer little or no benefit on the insular territories of the Caribbean. I will proceed by looking at the political and economic character of the territories, the resources of the Caribbean Sea, and the traditional or existing Law of the Sea and will conclude with an assessment and evaluation from the emerging law as contained in the Draft Convention under reference.

## The Caribbean: its political and economic character

The insular Caribbean consists of territories at varying stages of political development and evolution. There are, on the one hand, the independent states of Barbados, Cuba, Dominica, Dominican Republic, Grenada, Haiti, Jamaica, St. Lucia, St. Vincent and the Grenadines, and Trinidad and Tobago and, on the other, the nonindependent territories or dependencies of continental or extracontinental metropolitan powers: Antigua, Anguilla, Montserrat, British Virgin Islands, Cayman and Turks and Caicos islands (United Kingdom); Guadaloupe and Martinique (France); Puerto Rico, U.S. Virgin Islands, and Navassa Island (United States); Aves (Venezuela); and the Netherlands Antilles (The Netherlands). Some 23 separate administrations exist in this archipelago. The Associated States of Antigua and St. Kitts–Nevis will soon attain independent status. [Antigua and Barbuda became independent on 1 November 1981.—Ed.]

Economically, most of these territories are underdeveloped; a few of the least developed countries in the world are to be found in the Caribbean chain. These can be characterized as territories small in size with high population density, high unemployment, a low level of social services, and limited or nonexistent land-based natural resources. As a result, they lack the vital resource base for industrial development. Historically, their economies have been dependent upon agriculture, one crop in particular (sugarcane), which they have had to market in Europe or in North America. This pattern of dependence persists.[7] Moreover, terms of trade for their products, which have always been adverse, have steadily deteriorated, leaving the economies of most of the islands in a state of continuing instability and, in some cases, utter stagnation.

## The Caribbean Sea and its resources

In its topography, the Caribbean Sea is a semienclosed sea,[8] lying roughly between 10° and 20° N latitude and between 60° and 90° W longitude. It has about 2.6 million sq. km. of surface area and is enclosed by and separated from open ocean by continental or insular land masses for about three-quarters of its circumference. The maximum dimension of the sea, measured in an east-west direction, is nearly 1,800 miles, while the central axis extends slightly less than 900 miles.[9] It is a suboceanic basin with an average depth of about 2,700 meters.

The "geographic" continental shelf bordering most of the Caribbean is narrow. (It may in fact average out at the 200-meter isobath.) The average width is approximately 10 to 15 miles; the maximum is nearly everywhere less than 30 miles.[10] Only adjacent to the southwest coast of Cuba and to the northeast of the lowland coast of Honduras and Nicaragua does an extensive "geographic" continental shelf prevail, extending to a maximum width of roughly 125 miles. The continental slope throughout the Caribbean is steep, and the continental rise occupies a considerable area of the sea floor.

A knowledge of the resources of the sea is necessary for any evaluation or assessment of benefits to be derived by insular Caribbean territories from the emerging Law of the Sea. It would appear from available data that, in resources, the Caribbean Sea is no North Sea. In certain parts, however, it possesses exploitable living and nonliving resources of some worth. These resources tend to cling to the continental mainland.

With respect to living resources, the Caribbean Sea can be labeled an area of low productivity compared to the waters of the North Atlantic, where rich nutrient salts from deep layers are returned to the surface regularly by convectional overturns. Though small, some areas of rich local fisheries do exist. One is on the Venezuelan coast near Isla Margarita, around which occurs the natural incidence of the upwelling of nutrient-rich, deep-ocean waters, similar to Peru's Humboldt Current. Phytoplankton production, the primary source of marine life, is very high along the coastal waters of northwest Colombia and Venezuela, between the mainland and offshore islands. Some rich areas, however, are situated in the waters beyond this zone, particularly along the near shores of Costa Rica and Panama, close to the Bay Islands, and along a belt stretching from Yucatan eastward to envelop Cuba.[11] It is to be noted that most of these areas do not extend farther than 50 miles from the coasts of the nearest mainland or islands. Further, the waters around the insular Caribbean are not well endowed with living marine resources, due largely to the fact that the net sum of nutrients found in the waters off these islands seems to be greater in the South Equatorial Drift than in the North Equatorial Drift. The South Drift carries with it effluents from the Amazon, the Orinoco, and the river systems of Cayenne, Suriname, and Guyana. Since the nutrient levels in the water influence fish production, the areas influenced by the South Equatorial Drift (Trinidad and Tobago and areas possibly as far north as St. Lucia) are slightly more productive than those influenced by the North Equatorial Drift (Jamaica, Haiti, Dominican Republic, Puerto Rico, and the Leeward Islands).

Most of the Caribbean Sea is occupied by sedimentary formations, which are usually favorable to the accumulation of petroleum and gas deposits. The exceptions to the sedimentary basins of the Caribbean are the Central American isthmus and the Antillean archipelago (though Barbados and Trinidad are sedimentary) and the Cayman ridge and the midsea deep, which are of volcanic origin—a geological formation not usually associated with hydrocarbon deposits.[12] In view of the fact that a fair indicator of potential marine mineral deposits is the presence of such deposits on adjacent land masses, the areas offshore that are likely to produce oil and gas in commercially exploitable quantities would be east of the Yucatan peninsula, offshore Colombia and Venezuela, and in the submarine areas adjacent to Trinidad. The northwestern Caribbean Sea is known to contain petroleum deposits, possibly in commercial quantities off Cuba's shores.

In respect of hard and other minerals, on present indications, there appear to exist in the Caribbean undetermined quantities of manganese nodules and manganese dioxide concretions (possibly containing small amounts of copper, nickel, cobalt, and manganese); iron ore, titanium, and anhydrite, as well as surface deposits of metallic minerals such as zircan, ilmenite, monosite, chromite, and hematite; sand gravel and lime shells; and chemical precipitates, including phosphorite, phosphatic rock, red clays, and berite modular concretions. Titanium deposits are found to exist offshore south of Jamaica and Haiti. Surface deposits of manganese nodules have been discovered 200 miles west of Grenada, St. Lucia, and Martinique; north of Lake Maracaibo, Colombia, and Panama; and to the northeast of Honduras and the Yucatan peninsula. The Caribbean Sea is not known to be rich in these deposits, which lie on the sea and ocean floor, most prolifically in an area of the Pacific called the Clarion-Clipperton zone. Knowledge of the resources of the area remains fragmentary, though, and considerably more research and exploration need to be done to pinpoint and evaluate mineral deposits in the Caribbean.

For the insular territories, the sea itself is the major Caribbean resource, particularly when one considers that tourism based on sun, sea, and sand contributes significantly to the gross national product of most Caribbean territories—hence the concern of these territories for the preservation of the marine environment. The Caribbean Sea remains vulnerable to pollution. The executive director of the United Nations Environment Program (UNEP) has observed that, while the pollution problems of the Caribbean Sea may not have reached the magnitude of those in the Baltic and the Mediterranean, the similar landlocked configuration of the Caribbean with its potential for the retention of pollutants from a developing region warrants early protective action.[13]

In view of the heavy maritime traffic that passes through the sea and its straits, the pollution threat is ever present. Since the Caribbean is a major oil-producing and -refining region, oil tanker traffic is ever on the increase. A collision between two oil tankers in the Grenada passage seriously threatened Tobago, Isla Margarita, and even areas as far away as Mexico's Yucatan pen-

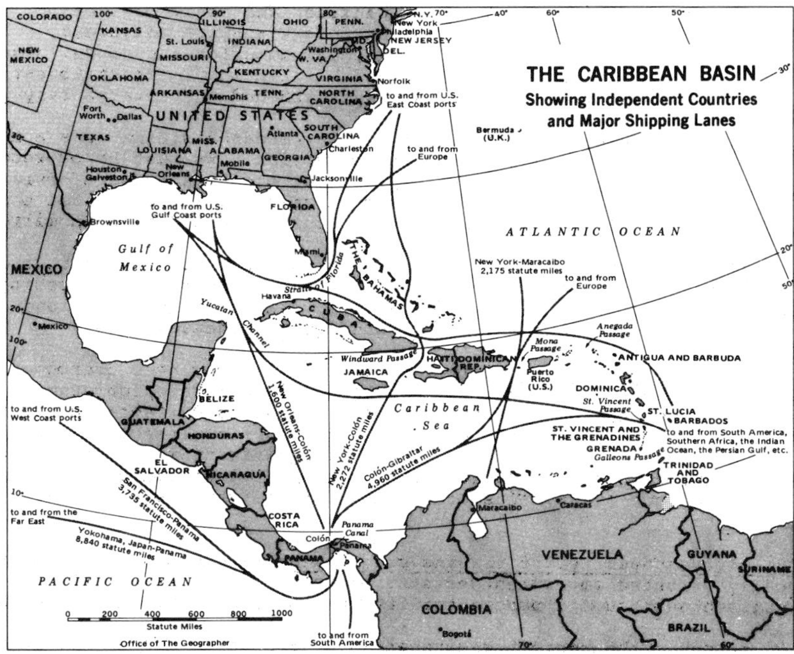


insula.[14] The Yucatan Channel (191 km.) between Mexico and Cuba is only one of five major international straits that give access to the Caribbean Sea. The other major trade routes are the Windward Passage (the most active Atlantic-Caribbean route, 83 km. wide) between Cuba and Haiti; the Mona Passage (61 km. wide) between the Dominican Republic and Puerto Rico; the Anegada Passage (89 km. wide) between the island of Anegada in the British Virgin Islands and the island of Sombrero (a dependency of the Associated State of Antigua); and the St. Vincent Passage (42 km. wide) between St. Lucia and St. Vincent. Movement through such narrow straits[15] by foreign military vessels, in addition to oil tankers and LNG vessels, is likely to impinge upon the security of the insular territories as well as pose serious threats to their sensitive and fragile marine ecosystems.

## The traditional law of the sea

The traditional legal order in the seas and oceans of the world was based on narrow belts of territorial sea adjacent to the coast, in which the coastal state exercised complete sovereignty with full civil, criminal, and administrative jurisdiction, with the exception of the right of innocent passage for the vessels of other states. Beyond this narrow belt of ocean space, all states enjoyed the freedom of the high seas. This freedom did not, however, attach to the seabed.[16] The first United Nations Conference on the Law of the Sea (UNCLOS I) ratified a system of ocean law and policy that had been largely shaped by developed nations. It gave some form of legitimacy to the continental shelf concept; this concept had been evolving in the wake of the unilateral Truman Declaration of 1945, which sought to appropriate for the United States the resources of the seabed and subsoil of the marine areas adjacent to its coast. From UNCLOS I emerged the following four conventions: the Convention on the Territorial Sea and Contiguous Zone; the Convention on the High Seas; the Convention on Fishing and Conservation of the Living Resources of the High Seas; and the Convention on the Continental Shelf. Only the Convention on the High Seas is said to be "generally declaratory of established principles of international law," but the other three provide evidence of the generally accepted rules bearing on their subject matter, the cogency of which depends in part on the number of ratifications to the conventions.[17]

The four 1958 Geneva conventions recognized four marine areas under coastal state sovereignty or jurisdiction: internal waters, territorial sea, contiguous zone, and continental shelf. Article 1 of the 1958 Geneva Convention on the Territorial Sea and Contiguous Zone provides that the "sovereignty of a state extends beyond its internal waters, to a belt of sea adjacent to its coast, described as the territorial sea."[18] Article 5 of the same convention states that "waters on the landward side of the baseline of the territorial sea form part of the internal waters of the State."[19] Article 24 of that convention says in part that "in a zone of the high seas contiguous to its territorial sea, the coastal state may exercise the control necessary to: (a) prevent . . . infringement of its customs, fiscal, immigration or sanitary regulations within its territory or territorial sea."[20] Paragraph 2 of that article stipulates that the contiguous zone "may not extend beyond twelve miles from the baseline from which the breadth of the territorial sea is measured." The convention provides, therefore, for a 12-mile belt of territorial sea and contiguous zone falling respectively under the coastal state's sovereignty and jurisdiction.

The 1958 Geneva Convention on the Continental Shelf states in Article 2 that the coastal state exercises over its continental shelf sovereign rights (to be distinguished from the "sovereignty" exercised in the territorial sea) for the purpose of exploring it and exploiting its natural resources.[21] The rights of the coastal state over the continental shelf do not affect the legal status of the superjacent waters as high seas or that of the air space above those waters.

The 1958 Geneva Convention on the High Seas defines the term "high seas" to mean all parts of the sea that are not included in the territorial sea or in the internal waters of a state.[22] In addition, it lays down that freedom of the high seas comprises, inter alia, both for coastal and noncoastal states, freedom of navigation, freedom of fishing, freedom to lay submarine cables and pipelines, and freedom to fly over the high seas.[23] Interestingly enough, the convention does not provide explicitly for freedom of marine scientific research. It deals in very general terms with marine pollution (Article 24) and puts an obligation on states to take measures to prevent pollution of the seas from dumping of radioactive waste (Article 25).[24]

The 1958 Geneva Convention on Fishing and Conservation of the Living Resources of the High Seas accords to all states the right for their nationals to engage in fishing on the high seas. It imposes as well on all states the duty to adopt, or to cooperate with other states in adopting, such measures as may be necessary for the conservation of the living resources of the high seas (Article 1(2)).[25] It also recognizes that a coastal state has a special interest in the maintenance of the productivity of the living resources in any area of the high seas adjacent to its territorial sea (Article 6(1)).[26] The convention imposes no firm obligations on states, nor does it establish any certain international regulations or standards for the preservation of the marine environment.

Of the insular Caribbean territories, only the Dominican Republic, Haiti, Jamaica, and Trinidad and Tobago are in their own right parties to the four 1958 Geneva conventions. Cuba is a signatory to all four conventions; the Dominican Republic and Haiti are parties to the 1958 Optional Protocol of Signature concerning the compulsory settlement of disputes.[27] It may be that the dependencies of the United States, the United Kingdom, France, and The Netherlands are subject to the legal regime elaborated in those conventions, as a result of the application of those conventions to their dependencies by the metropolitan powers on their becoming parties to the conventions. Applying the 1958 legal order of the oceans to the Caribbean Sea, coastal states exercise (1) sovereignty and jurisdiction over narrow belts of territorial seas and contiguous zones (not exceeding 12 miles) and (2) sovereign rights of exploration and exploitation over narrow continental shelves. In view of the fact that some 87 percent of the Caribbean is at depths below the 200-meter isobath, and given the criterion of depth-cum-exploitability as modified or limited by the notion of adjacency which defines the legal continental shelf in the 1958 Geneva Convention, much of the seabed and ocean floor of the Caribbean Sea falls, according to traditional law, outside of national jurisdiction.[28] Moreover, the waters of the Caribbean Sea lying beyond the territorial sea and contiguous zone have the character of high seas, to which the four freedoms (including the freedom to fish) are applicable. As a result, all nations, including insular Caribbean territories, had in traditional law, in the waters beyond the 3-mile or 12-mile territorial sea, a right for their nationals to fish freely as well as to enjoy the freedom of navigation and overflight. In addition, the 1958 Geneva Convention on the Territorial Sea and Contiguous Zone expressly prohibits the suspension of the innocent passage of foreign ships (including warships and oil tankers) through straits which are used for international navigation between one part of the high seas and another part of the high seas or the territorial sea of a foreign state.[29] As pointed out, access to the Caribbean Sea is afforded only through a number of international straits and passages situated between the islands of the archipelago. Further, it should be noted that passage is considered innocent so long as it is not prejudicial to the peace, good order, or security of the coastal state.[30]

## The emerging Law of the Sea

The 1958 Law of the Sea regime had some major drawbacks. It had been shaped by the major maritime powers in pursuit of their own interests in ocean space. None of these conventions received more than fifty-six ratifications or accessions. Precise limits of the territorial sea and of fisheries zones were left unresolved. The exploitability criterion in the definition of the continental shelf was open-ended, resulting in no precise or certain cutoff point for the outer limit of the continental shelf. The legal status of the submarine areas beyond the continental shelf was not addressed, nor was there any legal regime governing those areas. The conventions treated islands equally without distinguishing between island-states/territories and uninhabited or uninhabitable islands.

Claims by coastal states to appreciate their jurisdiction in the marine environment arose from the impact of marine technological advances and the rise since 1960 of many new states that were more concerned with controlling activities in marine areas and establishing exclusive rights to resources near their coasts than with the maintenance of the integrity of the high seas.[31] The technological advances that occurred between UNCLOS I (1958) and UNCLOS III (commencing 1974) gave man increased capabilities to exploit the resources of the continental shelf at greater ocean depths and distances from the coast, to engage intensively in ocean fishing, with the capacity to preserve and process catch, and to mine the deep sea bed as a result of the development of new mining technologies.[32] The questions to be properly addressed at this stage are, therefore, how UNCLOS III has dealt with these claims for expanding maritime jurisdictions and with the concerns of new as well as old states for controlling activities (with exclusive resource rights) in the marine areas adjacent to their coasts. A subsidiary but no less important question to be answered is the effect of the proposed legal regimes for ocean space on ocean wealth redistribution, particularly with reference to the insular Caribbean territories.

It is to be recalled that UNCLOS I recognized four marine areas under the sovereignty and jurisdiction of the coastal state. UNCLOS III increased these areas to six by the addition of "archipelagic waters" and the "exclusive economic zone." In respect of the regime of "archipelagic waters," Article I of the Draft Convention stipulates that the sovereignty of a coastal state extends beyond its land territory and internal waters and, *in the case of an archipelagic state, its archipelagic waters*, to an adjacent belt of sea described as the territorial sea.[33] An archipelagic state is defined as a state wholly constituted by one or more archipelagoes and may include islands; an archipelago means "a group of islands, including parts of islands, interconnecting waters and other natural features which are so closely interrelated that such islands, waters and other natural features, form an intrinsic geographical, economic and political entity, or which historically have been regarded as such."[34] The main advantage of a state designating itself to be an archipelagic state is that it is afforded an opportunity to draw straight archipelagic baselines joining the outermost points of the outermost islands and drying reefs of the archipelago subject to the condition that the ratio of the area of the water to the area of the land falls between 1 : 1 and 9 : 1.[35] It is from such baselines that the breadths of the territorial sea, the contiguous zone, the exclusive economic zone, and the continental shelf of an archipelagic state are measured, thereby allowing for a further extension seaward of the four traditional regimes. The archipelagic state regime, for the purpose of the exercise of the right of innocent passage by ships of all states, assimilates archipelagic waters to those of the territorial sea.

The regime of the exclusive economic zone confers on the coastal state sovereign rights for the purpose of exploring and exploiting, conserving and managing the natural resources, whether living or nonliving, of the seabed and subsoil and the superjacent waters, as well as sovereign rights with regard to other activities for the economic exploitation of the zone, such as the production of energy from the water, currents, and winds.[36] The regime also gives jurisdiction to the coastal state in respect of such other matters as marine scientific research, the protection and preservation of the marine environment, and the establishment and use of artificial islands, installations, and structures.[37] The breadth of the EEZ shall not extend beyond 200 nautical miles from the baselines from which the breadth of the territorial sea is measured.[38] The EEZ regime, at least for 200 nautical miles, is more comprehensive than the continental shelf regime, in that it embraces in its grasp nonliving as well as living resources of the seabed, subsoil, and water column.

In the emerging law of the Draft Convention, the territorial sea limit has been increased from 3 nautical miles to a uniform distance of 12 nautical miles from the applicable baselines. The contiguous zone, which in existing conventional law was fixed at 12 nautical miles, now extends up to 24 nautical miles from applicable baselines.[39] The continental shelf of coastal states can now, depending on its geological and geomorphological structure, extend beyond the 200-mile EEZ to the outer edge of the continental margin.[40] The convention proposes two alternative methods for establishing the outer edge of the continental margin, in cases where that margin extends beyond 200 miles. However, the outer limit drawn in accordance with either of the two methods laid down in Article 76 (4) of the Draft Convention cannot exceed either 350 nautical miles from the baselines from which the breadth of the territorial sea is measured or 100 nautical miles from the 2,500-meter isobath.[41]

## Assessment and evaluation

What appears clearly to be emerging from UNCLOS III is a shift in the balance of the present law of the sea from freedom for all states over the greater part of ocean space to control by coastal states over vast areas of what was previously high seas.[42] In short, UNCLOS III represents a substantial continuation of the extension of the national jurisdiction approach.[43] Even without further qualitative examination, it is evident that insular Caribbean territories cannot benefit spatially from that emerging law because they have short coastlines, lack substantial resources offshore, have narrow continental shelves, and possess little technological and financial capacity. Moreover, their position is made much worse by the fact that they front a semienclosed sea whose area is only 566,000 square nautical miles.

The extension seaward of the territorial sea results in the diminution of free fishing areas, since, under the traditional legal order, the seas outside the narrow belt of territorial sea were considered "high seas," in which the right for the nationals of all states to fish was legally recognized. In the context of the Caribbean Sea, only some states, off whose coasts fisheries of some worth are known to exist, are able to appropriate for their sole benefit the resources in areas of wider jurisdiction. The result is therefore a net loss of access to such areas for insular Caribbean territories, particularly since the areas around their coasts and in the mid-Caribbean are not considered rich fishing grounds.

It has been shown earlier that the application of the archipelagic concept will give archipelagic states wider maritime jurisdiction and possibly confer on them corresponding benefits. I am among those who have acknowledged the benefits that the application of the archipelagic regime to the insular Caribbean territories would confer on them.[44] I have argued that those territories constitute a historical archipelago entitling them, on the grounds of regional security, to delimit among themselves the waters of their archipelago in keeping with the concept. Luis Agrait states that, in a cramped archipelago such as the Caribbean, the establishment of a regional regime for the utilization of the sea and the exploration and conservation of its resources is imperative.[45] Rattray and others have said that the application of the archipelagic principle to the region would result in the closing of the waters between the island units, such waters being classified as either internal or territorial waters.[46] They have stated that the archipelagic principle cannot be applied to the whole of the multigovernmental archipelago. It can be applied, however, to a single group of islands, forming a single political entity of land territory and archipelagic waters of an island-state. The archipelagic regime would, then, apply to small archipelagic states, forming a political entity lying within the multigovernmental archipelago. Insular Caribbean states that seem to satisfy the criteria for archipelagic states, as laid down in the Draft Convention, include Antigua, St. Vincent and the Grenadines, Grenada, Trinidad and Tobago, and possibly Jamaica. These archipelagic island-states are in any event so close to each other, and to other islands in the chain, that they are likely to benefit only marginally from the application of the regime to themselves. Even though some advantages of the archipelagic concept for the insular Caribbean territories are readily acknowledged, the emerging Law of the Sea would appear to exclude the multigovernmental archipelago from its application.

An examination of the legal regime of the 200-nautical-mile EEZ, as it applies to the Caribbean Sea, reveals that no area of that sea falls outside of national jurisdiction. As a result, no area of high seas or deep sea bed attaching to an international regime lies therein. Because of the proximity of land territory, particularly in the insular archipelago, few of the territories can exercise sovereign rights over a full 200-nautical-mile EEZ in the Caribbean Sea.[47] It is roughly estimated that one state, Colombia, would have jurisdiction over some 20 percent of the entire Caribbean seabed, and Colombia, Mexico, and Venezuela together would control 37 percent. The four poorest states acquire 14.8 percent; the four metropolitan powers—France, The Netherlands, the United Kingdom, and the United States—secure rights to 19.5 percent of the Caribbean Sea, by virtue of their possessions or dependencies; Cuba would get 8 percent, Jamaica 8.8 percent, Haiti 3.6 percent, Dominican Republic 6 percent, the Leeward Islands 5.5 percent, the Windward Islands 13.7 percent, and Trinidad and Tobago 3 percent. With regard therefore to spatial distribution of the Caribbean Sea, the insular Caribbean territories find themselves at a serious disadvantage vis-à-vis the continental mainland territories, particularly Colombia and Venezuela.

With respect to spatial distribution of the Caribbean Sea, insular territories in the archipelago are further prejudiced by the presence of offshore islands, belonging to continental mainland countries, which are situated great distances from those countries and close to other states. One example is Aves (Birds) Island, over which Venezuela exercises sovereignty. Nweihed states that Aves Island is a modest extension of sand covered by purslane (500 by 150 meters maximum and 50 meters minimum), inhabited by birds and turtles which form a perfect ecological cycle: the turtles swim to the island from all around the Caribbean to lay their eggs, and the birds feed on the baby turtles and leave their droppings to form what used to be the main economic resource of Aves—guano.[48] It is interesting to note that Venezuela has declared a 200-mile EEZ around Aves island, which has a serious impact on the extent of exclusive economic zone that can be claimed by Puerto Rico, Guadeloupe, Dominica, Montserrat, and St. Kitts–Nevis. Nweihed has stated further that the Institute of Marine Technology and Science of Simón Bolívar University produced two hypothetical maps to illustrate what the EEZ of Venezuela would be with and without Aves Island—a difference that amounts to one-third of the total area. As a result of its sovereignty over Aves Island, Venezuela's gain is translated into a direct and substantial loss of ocean space, with the possible consequence of loss of access to living and nonliving resources, for the insular Caribbean territories of Puerto Rico, Guadeloupe, Dominica, Montserrat, and St. Kitts–Nevis. I hold strongly to the view that no basis exists in international customary or conventional law that would permit Venezuela to declare a 200-mile EEZ around Aves Island.[49]

Insofar as the living resources of the Caribbean Sea are concerned, the EEZ regime now effectively places the exploitation of those resources within the sole competence of the states that border on the sea. In view of the fact that the living resources of the Caribbean Sea that are commercially exploitable are to be found closer to the continental landmass than to the insular territories, those territories are now denied an access to resources that they have habitually had in traditional law. Such an access was necessary to assist those territories in providing nutrition and employment for their people, developing their fishing industries, and, in the process, expanding their economies. The Draft Convention seeks to provide access for landlocked and geographically disadvantaged states, but that access, which is an access to the surplus over and above that which the coastal state itself can harvest, is really no more than a privilege to be withdrawn at the discretion of the coastal (donor) state as its own expanding industry is able to utilize what may previously have been a surplus.[50] What is particularly disturbing is that the determination of whether a surplus exists rests subjectively and possibly capriciously with the donor state. The landlocked and geographically disadvantaged states have not, in the Draft Convention, secured the legal right to participate in the exploitation of the living resources beyond the territorial sea. All the insular territories in the archipelagic chain fall in the category of disadvantaged states.

The global inequity of the EEZ has been recognized. Arvid Pardo states that at least one-third of ocean space, by far the most valuable waters for economic uses and accessible resources, is placed under national jurisdiction and control.[51] He concludes that ten states obtain more than half the area which the Draft Convention proposes to place under national control, and six of these states are considered to be wealthy. This inequity is compounded in the case of the insular Caribbean states, which enjoyed access not only to the waters of the mainland territories of the Caribbean but also to those of states fronting the Atlantic seaboard, such as Brazil, Cayenne, Suriname, and Guyana. The fishing industries of Barbados and Trinidad and Tobago, which were dependent on access to those waters, have virtually died since meaningful access has been denied them. What seems to be desirable for the Caribbean is a system whereby the living resources would be subjected to a regional regime for both conservation and utilization, and bilateral arrangements for the reciprocal grant of fishing rights would be worked out among the states bordering the Caribbean Sea. Such an approach seems to provide the only means by which the insular Caribbean territories can derive any benefit from the application of the EEZ regime to the Caribbean Sea. While the Draft Convention raises pious hopes in this regard, it remains to be seen whether states bordering the Caribbean Sea will in good faith implement these provisions.[52]

In the emerging law, the continental shelf regime has really no practical relevance in the Caribbean Sea, since the EEZ regime confers on coastal states sovereign rights in respect of the nonliving resources to be found in the 200-nautical-mile zone. Moreover, because of the limited size and semienclosed nature of the Caribbean Sea, no areas of seabed lie outside the 200-mile EEZ to which the natural prolongation principle of the continental shelf can properly apply. The granting of sovereign rights to coastal states to explore and exploit areas extending beyond 200 nautical miles to the outer edge of the continental margin further erodes the international seabed area, from the exploitation of which insular Caribbean territories may have expected to derive benefits in keeping with the principle of the common heritage of mankind. Professor Hedberg holds the view that special regimes should apply to restricted seas like the Caribbean.[53] He says that the jurisdictional boundaries should be dealt with separately for the ocean surface (navigation), for the ocean water body (fishing), and for the ocean floor (mineral resources). Insular Caribbean territories may then continue to have the freedom to fish in the Caribbean Sea in areas beyond a 12-mile territorial sea limit, if such a jurisdictional boundary is established for fishing.

As pointed out, the Caribbean is a major artery of international commerce and navigation, with most of the straits giving access to it made up by the territorial sea or contiguous zone of bordering states. This gives rise to the twin problems of coastal state security and damage to the marine environment. The basic principle underlying the legal regime of straits used for international navigation is that the right of transit passage shall not be impeded or suspended. Ships and aircraft, in the exercise of the right of transit passage, are required to proceed without delay through or over the strait, to refrain from any threat or use of force against the sovereignty of states bordering the straits, to refrain from any activities other than those incidental to their normal modes of continuous and expeditious transit, and to comply with generally accepted international regulations, procedures, and practices for prevention, reduction, and control of pollution from ships. Nonetheless, there is no competence in the strait state to defend its sovereignty, territorial integrity, and political independence and to protect its marine environment through the prohibition or suspension of transit passage in straits bordering its coasts. Although the interest of the international community in freedom of navigation must be recognized, it cannot be done at the expense of denying to individual states, which may face the daily prospect of warships close to their shores or of nuclear-powered vessels or supertankers traversing their territorial seas and contiguous zones, the right to protect themselves from pollution threats or military confrontations near their shores. Relating this general concern of those Third World countries that border straits to the situation in the Caribbean, I have in another place, in advocating the application to the Caribbean of the *mare clausum* and archipelago concepts, felt that such application would have the beneficial effect of enhancing regional security by closing the

Caribbean Sea to the exercises and posturings of the armed fleets of the great powers.[54]

On the question of the preservation of the marine environment, it was stated that the insular Caribbean territories are particularly vulnerable to marine pollution, more so when note is taken of their growing dependence on the sea and its resources as basic ingredients for their fishing and tourist industries. The pollution threat arises largely from the fact that the Caribbean Sea is a major route for the movement of oil tankers to ports on the Gulf of Mexico and the eastern seaboard of the United States. The Draft Convention places a general obligation on states to protect and preserve the marine environment. States, acting through competent international organizations or general diplomatic conferences, are required to establish international rules and standards for the prevention, reduction, and control of pollution of the marine environment from vessels and to promote the adoption likewise of routing systems designed to avoid accidents. States are required to make such international rules and standards applicable to vessels flying their flags. In respect of pollution control, due publicity must be given to any particular requirements laid down by states for the entry of foreign vessels into their ports or internal waters. Laws and regulations adopted for pollution prevention, reduction, and control shall not, however, hamper the innocent passage of foreign vessels. The Draft Convention allows coastal states to adopt special mandatory measures for special areas of their EEZS, provided that such higher pollution standards are justified and agreed to by the competent international organization.

The coastal state is empowered under the Draft Convention to institute proceedings against a foreign vessel when that vessel is voluntarily within a port or at an offshore terminal of that state in respect of a violation occurring within its territorial sea or EEZ. It may also institute proceedings against a vessel navigating in its territorial sea which has during its passage violated its laws and regulations. Further, it may institute proceedings against a vessel navigating in the EEZ or territorial sea when that vessel has in the EEZ violated its laws and regulations that conform and give effect to applicable international rules and standards.[55] Proceedings can be initiated, however, only if the violation has resulted in a discharge causing major damage or a threat of major damage to the coastline, resources, or related interests of the coastal state.

The evolving law of the sea deals much more comprehensively than UNCLOS I with the subject of the protection and preservation of the marine environment. As stated, UNCLOS I devoted only two articles in the High Seas Convention to the subject (Articles 24 and 25). It is felt that the new law does provide the insular Caribbean territories with the necessary legal powers to institute proceedings against foreign vessels that pollute marine areas under their sovereignty and jurisdiction—indeed an evident benefit from the emerging law. Whether these territories are in a position to monitor for pollution of the environment all foreign vessels traversing their maritime zones is in serious doubt since few of them possess any sizable long-range air or naval reconnaissance capability. As a result, even where provisions exist to enable insular Caribbean territories to combat pollution, their capability to do so is extremely limited. Those territories will therefore have to rely on the major maritime powers to ensure that acceptable international pollution standards are rigorously applied to vessels flying the flags of those powers.

In view of the inequities arising worldwide as a result of the expansion of national maritime jurisdiction, particularly in the semienclosed Caribbean Sea, it is necessary to examine the proposed international regime for the exploration and exploitation of the area and its resources beyond national jurisdiction to determine whether through that regime some kind of global equity can be restored to the overall package of emerging Law of the Sea proposals.

Part XI of the Draft Convention, in the section entitled Principles Governing the Area, states, *inter alia*, that the area and its resources are the common heritage of mankind.[56] This principle is considered to be a peremptory norm of general international law. To give effect to this principle, UNCLOS III has elaborated a "parallel system" for the exploitation of manganese nodules (rich in copper, cobalt, nickel, and manganese) which lie on the ocean floor and in prolific quantities in the area of the Pacific Ocean known as the Clarion-Clipperton zone. Under the parallel system, access is afforded to state parties, state enterprises, and natural and juridical persons to exploit the resources of the area. In addition, however, UNCLOS III has also decided to establish the enterprise as an organ of the future International Seabed Authority. The enterprise will engage in direct exploitation of the manganese nodules either on its own or in joint ventures. Direct exploitation of these nodules by developing countries in association with the authority is also provided for in the Draft Convention. At present and in the foreseeable future, only a few industrialized countries have the financial and technological capability to exploit deep sea bed mineral resources. It is questionable whether the proposed international regime and machinery will redress the present imbalance in the opportunities for exploitation of the seabeds by states. This imbalance is particularly evident in the case of developing countries which have, by and large, neither the technological nor the financial capability for such exploitations.

The question of technology transfer has been difficult to negotiate, given the reluctance of possessors of technology to transfer seabed mining technology to the enterprise and to developed as well as developing countries. Developing countries have sought to include in the text of the Draft Convention provisions that would make mandatory the transfer of technology to the enterprise and developing countries. On the other hand, the developed, industrialized countries possessing the technology favored the voluntary, open-market approach. The text resulting from long and arduous negotiations in UNCLOS III contains features of both these approaches. While the relevant provision in the Draft Convention appears to be generally satisfactory to the socialist countries of Eastern Europe and to the developing countries in the Group of 77, the industrialized countries, mainly West Germany, Japan, and the United States, remain firmly opposed to that aspect of the technology transfer provisions which would require deep sea bed mining contractors to undertake the same obligation in respect of technology transfer to developing countries as they are prepared to undertake for the enterprise, the mining arm of the future International Seabed Authority, and this is so despite the strict conditions attached to such a transfer.[57] The availability of skilled personnel in developing countries represents a further limiting factor, although the convention does place an obligation on the contractor to draw up practical programs for the training of personnel of developing countries, including their participation in all activities covered by the mining contract.[58]

As regards the financing of the exploitation of deep sea bed minerals by developing countries, there is no provision in the Draft Convention dealing with this subject. In this connection, it will be recalled that the cost of exploiting a single mine site (that is, mining, transporting, and processing) is likely to be in the vicinity of U.S.$1 billion. Few developing countries are in a position to invest such a large sum in deep sea bed mineral exploitation, and several of those that can are already faced with growing foreign debt burdens. It can be reasonably concluded that, although the text does in theory envisage direct participation by developing countries in the exploitation of manganese nodules, in practical terms a deep sea bed exploitation remains clearly out of the reach of most, if not all, developing countries. Accordingly, developing countries as a group, and insular Caribbean territories in particular, are as a result of the Draft Convention in no position to exploit the hard minerals of the deep sea bed. Wealth from the exploitation of the seabed will thus accrue primarily, if not exclusively, to corporations and national treasuries of the industrialized countries. While it is expected that corporations engaged in seabed mineral exploitation will be required to pay taxes to the authority on the profits of the mining sector of their operations, the revenues to be derived therefrom are to meet a host of commitments, including the administrative costs of the secretariat as well as monetary compensation to land-based producers of seabed minerals, who may be adversely affected by seabed production.[59] What remains from those profits appears hardly likely to make a noticeable dent in the kind of international economic assistance that is universally acknowledged as required for bringing about the economic and social development of developing countries, particularly the insular Caribbean archipelagic territories. Consequently, one of the main objectives that led to the convening of UNCLOS III—a desire to prevent the industrialized countries from monopolizing deep sea bed resources—will not be achieved.

It was also the hope of many that the international regime would provide an institutional structure, in which all countries would be able to participate in the management of the resources of the area. The emerging international regime envisages an assembly comprising all states parties, a council of thirty-six in which various special interests are represented, and a secretariat. The Draft Convention designates the council as the executive organ of the authority, leaving to the assembly the power to formulate general policies. Virtually any action of substance that the assembly is called upon to take is fed to it by the council. In sum, the management of the area will be in the hands of the council. Although the Group of 77 can expect to be well represented on the council, holding even as many as twenty-four seats, it must be recognized that decisions on the most crucial aspects of the council's work are to be taken either by a three-fourths majority or by consensus. This factor denies developing countries any effective role in managing the affairs of the council.

Given their size and stage of development, and bearing in mind that they do not fall among any of the "special interest" groups to be represented in the council, it is unlikely that the insular Caribbean territories (as members of the wider Group of 77) will in the foreseeable future be in a position to engage in deep sea bed mineral exploitation or will ever be elected to the thirty-six-member council. Moreover, since the insular Caribbean territories, with the possible exception of Haiti and Dominica, are not considered by the United Nations to be hard-core underdeveloped countries, they will rank far down on the list of developing countries entitled to receive financial benefits and assistance from revenues of the International Seabed Authority. The possibility does exist that qualified nationals of the insular Caribbean territories may gain employment either with the secretariat (the seat of which will be in Jamaica) or with the enterprise. This is likely to accelerate the brain drain at a time when technicians and professionals of that type are required for the economic development of the insular Caribbean territories themselves. Quite apart from the fact that Caribbean territories will gain little from the international regime, a real possibility exists that Caribbean land-based producers of seabed minerals, such as Cuba, are likely to be adversely affected by seabed mining. On the whole, therefore, the benefits to be derived by the insular Caribbean from the international regime appear to be marginal.

## Concluding remarks

I agree with the late Eric Williams that the emerging Law of the Sea represents for the insular Caribbean territories nothing short of disaster. While the proposals in the Draft Convention do confer expanded national jurisdiction on coastal states and, *a fortiori*, on the insular Caribbean territories, the known resources, both living and nonliving, to be found in the marine areas embraced by such expanded jurisdictions are in the case of the Caribbean so minimal as not even to justify their declaration of EEZs at this time. The only apparent advantage accruing to the insular Caribbean territories from the international recognition of the EEZ is the jurisdiction that it confers on coastal states in respect of pollution matters, thereby allowing them, in certain defined circumstances, to institute proceedings against foreign vessels that have caused pollution damage to their marine environment.

Insofar as the international regime is concerned, the insular Caribbean territories are unlikely to possess the financial or technological capability to engage in deep sea bed mineral production. Further, they do not seem to have the political will to do so, since their economies are by and large not based on an industrialization program that would require inputs of manganese, copper, nickel, and cobalt. These countries, already woefully short of skilled technicians and professionals for their own limited industrialization efforts, are hardly likely to encourage their nationals to seek training and employment in the deep sea bed mining industry, as this would further exacerbate the already serious brain drain from developing to industrialized countries. Although the insular Caribbean territories, as members of the international authority, will be afforded the opportunity to express opinions in the assembly and to vote for general policies to be adopted therein, they will face obstacles in getting elected to the council, the executive organ of the authority. The financial benefits accruing from the exploitation of mankind's common heritage to which they are entitled by right are not likely to be of a magnitude necessary to assist those countries in any meaningful way with their economic and social development. Finally, the inability of those territories to deny access to foreign vessels through the various straits that lead into the Caribbean Sea will mean that their sea remains open for the military exercises and posturings of the navies of the great powers, with all the attendant harmful effects on national and regional security.

The only salvation for insular Caribbean territories appears to lie in the fashioning of a regional approach within the context of the global Law of the Sea by all the countries of the wider Caribbean Basin, including the Gulf of Mexico and possibly the areas adjacent to the Caribbean (the ocean swamp area stretching from Brazil to Guyana where some Caribbean territories have traditionally and habitually fished). Such a regional approach would provide, *inter alia*, for (1) equitable participation in the exploitation of the living resources of the Caribbean and adjacent regions, utilizing in a rational way the available capital and fishing technology, including fish-processing plants located in the countries of the region; (2) safety of international navigation in the Caribbean Sea, particularly in respect of oil tankers; (3) control and abatement of pollution from all sources, together with regional joint contingency planning against pollution and the threat thereof; (4) regional security of the coastal states; (5) cooperative programs in the conduct of marine scientific research; and (6) joint ventures in the exploration and exploitation of the resources of the region. To this end a second specialized conference[60] of Caribbean states should be convened following the conclusion of UNCLOS III for the purpose of translating the new Law of the Sea that has emerged into a regional accord, which will, we hope, ensure the equitable conferral of benefits on the peoples of countries that front the sea and more particularly on the poor peoples of the insular Caribbean archipelago.

## Notes

1. ERIC WILLIAMS, THREAT TO THE CARIBBEAN COMMUNITY 30 (1975).

2. *Id.* at 23. The CDCC of ECLA met in Havana from 31 October to 4 November 1975 and discussed Law of the Sea questions but reached no common coordinated position. No further meetings on a special equitable regime for the Caribbean appear to have been held.

3. For a detailed discussion of the concept, *see* LENNOX F. BALLAH, *Applicability of the Archipelago and Mare Clausum Concepts to the Caribbean Sea*, in PACEM IN MARIBUS: CARIBBEAN STUDY AND DIALOGUE 276–304 (1974).

4. *See* K. O. RATTRAY, A. KIRTON, AND P. ROBINSON, *The Effect of the Existing Law of the Sea on the Development of the Caribbean Region and the Gulf of Mexico*, in PACEM IN MARIBUS, *supra* note 3, at 256–57, for a discussion of the concept.

5. A large majority of states at UNCLOS III have supported the EEZ; fifty-six

states have declared 200-mile exclusive economic zones, and twenty-three others have 200-mile fishing zones; many others have such legislation under consideration. In addition, fourteen have declared 200-mile territorial seas. *See* The Geographer, U.S. Dept. of State, LIMITS IN THE SEAS, no. 36 (4th rev. 1982).

6. DRAFT TREATY ON THE LAW OF THE SEA (INFORMAL TEXT), UN Doc. A/Conf.62/WP.10/Rev.3, reproduced in 19 INT'L LEGAL MATERIALS 1129 (1980) (hereinafter cited as Draft Treaty).

7. W. CARTEY, THE WESTERN INDIES, ISLANDS IN THE SUN 185 (1967).

8. LEWIS M. ALEXANDER, SPECIAL CIRCUMSTANCES: SEMI-ENCLOSED SEAS, PROCEEDINGS OF LAW OF SEA INSTITUTE, EIGHTH ANNUAL CONFERENCE 201–15 (1974).

9. R. D. HODGSON, *The American Mediterranean: One Sea, One Region?*, paper presented at the Workshop on Regional Institutions for Marine Management in the Gulf and Caribbean. Simón Bolívar University, Caracas (February 1972).

10. *Id.*

11. *Id.*

12. V. E. MCKELVEY AND F. F. WANG, WORLD SUBSEA MINERAL RESOURCES (1969).

13. An article entitled *Meetings on Endangered Caribbean Environment*, Diplomatic World Bulletin, 23 February 1981, at 3.

14. See report in New York Times, 22 July 1979, at 1; the two vessels involved were the *Aegean Captain* and the *Atlantic Empress*, with capacities of 100,000 tons and 90,000 tons, respectively. The accident took place at 7:00 P.M. on 19 July 1979, approximately 50 km. northeast of Tobago. The two tankers, under apparent Greek ownership, were registered in Monrovia, Liberia.

15. ALEXANDER, *supra* note 8, at 209. Other straits and passages are the Dominica Passage between Guadeloupe (France) and Dominica; the Martinique Channel between Dominica and Martinique (France); the St. Lucia Channel between Martinique (France) and St. Lucia. Note that the Yucatan and Grenada passages are the only two straits that afford access through EEZS; other trade routes are through territorial waters and contiguous zones.

16. PATRICIA BIRNIE, *Searching for a New Law of the Sea, Commonwealth Interests on* UNCLOS III, in ROUND TABLE, no. 264, at 350–69 (1976).

17. IAN BROWNLIE, BASIC DOCUMENTS IN INTERNATIONAL LAW 68 (1972).

18. 516 UNTS 205 at 206.

19. *Id.* at 210.

20. *Id.* at 220.

21. 499 UNTS 311 at 312.

22. 450 UNTS 11 at 82.

23. Article 2, *id.* at 82–84.

24. *Id.* at 96.

25. 559 UNTS 285 at 288.

26. *Id.* at 290.

27. Multilateral Treaties in Respect of which the Secretary-General Performs De-

positary Functions, UN Doc. ST/LEG/Ser.D/13 at 587 (1979).

28. Alexander, *supra* note 8, at 204, 205.

29. Article 16(4), 516 UNTS 205 at 216.

30. Article 14(4), *id.* at 214.

31. ARVID PARDO, *The Evolving Law of the Sea: A Critique of the Informal Composite Negotiating Text*, 1 OCEAN Y. B. 9 (1977).

32. ROBERT H. MANLEY, *Developing Nation Imperatives for a New Law of the Sea*, 7 OCEAN DEV. & INT'L L. 11 (1979).

33. Draft Treaty, 19 INT'L LEGAL MATERIALS 1147 (1980).

34. Art. 46, *id.* at 1160.

35. Art. 47(1), *id.*

36. Art. 56(1)(a), *id.* at 1163.

37. Art. 56(1)(b), *id.*

38. Art. 57, *id.*

39. Art. 33(2), *id.* at 1156.

40. Art. 76(1), *id.* at 1172.

41. Art. 76(5), *id.*

42. PARDO, *supra* note 31, at 11.

43. MANLEY, *supra* note 32, at 13.

44. *See* LUIS E. AGRAIT, UNCLOS III *and Non-Independent States*, 7 OCEAN DEV. & INT'L L. 22 (1979); *see also* Ballah, *supra* note 3, at 297.

45. Agrait, *supra* note 44, at 22.

46. Rattray, Kirton, and Robinson, *supra* note 4, at 256.

47. For a lucid exposition of approximate entitlements of Caribbean states in percentages vis-à-vis the theoretical expectations of a 200-mile EEZ, *see* Williams, *supra* note 1. These percentages were apparently worked out prior to delimitation agreements.

48. KALDONE G. NWEIHED, *"EZ" (Uneasy) Delimitation in the Semi-Enclosed Caribbean Sea: Recent Agreements between Venezuela and her Neighbors*, 8 OCEAN DEV. & INT'L L. 21 (1980).

49. JORGE CASTAÑEDA, *The Patrimonial Sea as a Regional Concept*, in PACEM IN MARIBUS: A SELECTION FROM DIALOGUE AT PREPARATORY CONFERENCE 353 (1972). Castañeda argues that since the patrimonial sea is not a zone of territorial sovereignty but a zone of limited economic jurisdiction, uninhabited islands would not enjoy a patrimonial sea. *See also* Art. 121(3) of Draft Convention, 19 INT'L LEGAL MATERIALS 1184 (1980).

50. For definition, *see* Art. 70(2), Draft Treaty, 19 INT'L LEGAL MATERIALS 1169 (1980).

51. PARDO, *supra* note 31, at 25.

52. Art. 70(3), Draft Treaty, 19 INT'L LEGAL MATERIALS 1169–70 (1980).

53. HOLLIS B. HEDBERG, *Ocean Floor Boundaries*, 204 SCIENCE 136 (1979).

54. *See* Ballah, *supra* note 3, at 206.

55. *See* Arts. 218 and 220 Draft Treaty, 19 INT'L LEGAL MATERIALS 1222–23 (1980).

56. Art. 136, *id.* at 1187.

57. Art. 5(3)(e) of Annex III, *id.* at 1255. The transfer is to be on fair and reasonable commercial terms.

58. Art. 15, Annex III, *id.* at 1267–68.

59. Art. 13, Annex III, *id.* at 1261–67, for the financial terms of contracts.

60. The First Specialized Conference of Caribbean Countries on Problems of the Sea was held at Santo Domingo from 31 May to 9 June 1972. The Declaration of Santo Domingo recognized the principle of the 200-mile patrimonial sea. For the text *see* UN Doc. A/AC. 138/80, reproduced in 66 AM. J. INT'L L. 918 (1972).

# Fishery Interests of the United States in the Caribbean

*Clarence P. Idyll*

THE UNITED STATES has several fishery interests in the Caribbean, the most important of which are the Caribbean as a fishing area, as a market for seafood, as a source of imports of seafoods, and as a locale for fishery and oceanographic research.

The Caribbean Sea can be delimited in several ways. Geographically it is a semienclosed part of the Atlantic Ocean, bounded on the south and west by South and Central America and Mexico, on the north by the Greater Antilles (the islands of Cuba, Jamaica, Hispaniola, and Puerto Rico), and on the east by a great sweeping chain of islands, the Lesser Antilles, stretching from the Virgin Islands to Grenada. Politically the Caribbean exhibits bewildering complexity and variety, including continental countries of Central and South America (some very large) and island countries (some very small). The history of many of these countries includes colonialism under Great Britain, Spain, France, or The Netherlands, but most of them are now independent. There are U.S.-associated commonwealth and territories, Puerto Rico and the Virgin Islands, in the region.

For the purpose of this discussion, three countries on the shoulder of South America, which are geographically outside the Caribbean, are included because of their close ties with the region's fisheries: Guyana, Suriname, and Cayenne. For the same reason the Bahamas are also included as part of the Caribbean.

## The Caribbean as a fishing area

The amount of fish available for capture in the Caribbean is circumscribed by the physical-biological characteristics of its seas and by the changing political control of the world's oceans. The whole of the region (except the Bahamas) is within the tropics, and, as a result, its oceanic waters produce less commercially valuable products per unit area than those in the temperate zone. The basic productivity of the area may not be significantly less than that of some temperate zone waters, if annual rates of plankton production are considered, but the production is spread over the whole year instead of occurring in short seasonal blooms. This has the effect of supporting smaller quantities of animal plankton and, consequently, fewer exploitable large fish and invertebrates farther up the biological chain.

The lack of seasonal maxima in phytoplankton production in the Caribbean is a consequence of thermal stability. Except in some small local areas, a warm layer of surface water persists above the thermocline, with cooler, nutrient-laden water beneath. In the temperate zone these nutrients are overturned seasonally as the water cools, triggering a blooming of plant life that starts the biological wheel spinning. Without this injection of nutrients into the surface photic zone where plants can grow, Caribbean surface waters remain relatively unproductive.

A second physical reason why Caribbean waters exhibit smaller productivity of commercially valuable fishery species is that shallow areas are relatively scarce. Half the water area of the region is over 2,000 fathoms deep and four-fifths over 1,000 fathoms. The deepest part of the Caribbean is the Cayman Trench (25,216 ft.), and the deepest part of the Atlantic, the Puerto Rican Trench (30,184 ft.), is in the Caribbean area. Most of the islands, and to a considerable extent even the continental countries of the region, have steep-to shores with narrow shelves. This has a direct effect on the quantities of fish that can be supported, since it is in the shallow regions that nutrients accumulate and that light can penetrate to support photosynthetic production of plant material.

Thus, compared with the great fishery grounds of the world, the Caribbean supports fewer fish. Nonetheless, it is far from barren. Our beliefs about its true potential have swung back and forth a number of times. The water areas of the region are immense—800,000 to 1.5 million square nautical miles, depending on what is included, and 1,600 miles wide by 400 to 600 miles long. It seems logical to suppose that this much water should have huge quantities of fish. This supposition seems to be supported by the swarms of fish that occupy coral reefs and the very large schools of tunas, flying fishes, and other species that are sometimes seen. But according to surveys undertaken in the 1940s by the United States Fish and Wildlife Service, the region was poor in fish and there was little point in looking for unused resources. In the 1950s further surveys by U.S. exploratory fishing vessels revealed that the earlier pessimism had been exaggerated and that commercially valuable stocks of shrimp and of some species of fish do exist in the region. It appeared that tuna might be abundant enough to support profitable fisheries. Influenced in part by this, residents of the region, as well as foreigners, began to look to the Caribbean as a potential source of great fisheries wealth.

It was partly this hope and expectation that stimulated a major survey by the Food and Agriculture Organization (FAO) funded by the United Nations Development Program (UNDP). The survey, from 1965 to 1971, increased greatly the existing knowledge of Caribbean fishery resources and methods of producing and marketing them. Following a large number of fishing trials (2,500 ship-days at sea), the surveyors could identify with reasonable confidence the size of the Caribbean fishery resource and the locations of concentrations. In general the conclusions of these extensive trials were that there are no large untapped resources in the Caribbean capable of supporting a sustained industrial-level fishery. This is not to say that more fish cannot be caught in some regions. In the years since the survey, many local fishermen have increased their catches and the efficiency of their operations. And substantial amounts of groundfish have been taken from the shelf off the Guyanas. The hope for a large-scale tuna fishery seems unrealistic, but Japanese and other tuna fleets operate to a limited degree in these waters. The FAO/UNDP survey did not claim to have the last word about the size of the exploitable fish stocks in so vast a region, but it would be hard to continue the belief that the Caribbean is an untapped source of huge resources.

## U.S. fisheries in the Caribbean

U.S. commercial fisheries have operated in the Caribbean for many decades, catching principally snappers, shrimp, and spiny lobsters. The snapper fishery goes back a century; the shrimp fishery has been extremely valuable; the lobster fishery has never been large, but the high demand for this product has made the fishery of special interest to Americans.

The opportunities for U.S. commercial fishermen in the Caribbean, and the conditions under which fishing can be done, have changed greatly during the past decade. This has been the consequence of changing concepts of marine law and the general extension of limits of national jurisdiction. When the snapper-grouper and shrimp fisheries were at their height in the region, the countries there claimed only 3-mile territorial seas, and many valuable fishing grounds were beyond that limit. Later some countries extended jurisdiction over fisheries to twelve miles. To fish legally in some of the most productive grounds, U.S. fishermen had to purchase licenses. Then many of the countries (including the United States) followed what had become a worldwide pattern by extending fisheries jurisdiction out to 200 miles, and what had been traditionally international waters were now closed to foreign fishing except under special arrangements.

U.S. recreational fishermen pursue a number of species in the Caribbean, including bluefin tuna, sharks, billfishes, snook, and tarpon. This activity increased greatly during the 1960s. American fishermen take part in tournaments in the Bahamas, Puerto Rico, the Virgin Islands, Jamaica, and other places. They also fish at private and commercial clubs on many of the islands and in Central America. While commercial fishing by Americans in the region has been declining, recreational fishing seems likely to continue to increase.

Shrimp has been by far the greatest target for the U.S. fishery in the Caribbean. At its height in 1973, the fishery supported 390 vessels in the three Guyanas, Trinidad, and Barbados and produced 20,000 tons of shrimp valued at $125 million. The U.S. shrimp fishery in the Caribbean started in Mexico in 1947 when vessels based in Tampa and other Florida ports began to operate on the Campeche Banks. These grounds, which at that time were outside territorial limits claimed by Mexico, were highly productive, and they helped support the rapid and profitable growth of the industry. Later U.S. vessels fished in several other Caribbean countries, including all of those off the coast of Central America, plus Colombia and Venezuela. Beginning in 1957, U.S. Fish and Wildlife Service exploratory fishing vessels caught large quantities of shrimp on the extensive shallows off the Guyanas, stimulating a large and lucrative fishery in which many U.S. vessels participated. That fishery still exists today but under substantially altered circumstances because of the political changes that have taken place.

These changes have also had a major impact on American shrimp fleets that had been operating off Mexico. In 1972 over 700 Texas and Florida vessels shrimped off its coast, landing an average of about 10 million pounds a year. In 1976, following the declaration by Mexico of an extension of its jurisdiction over fisheries to 200 miles, an agreement was signed between that country and the United States that provided for a phaseout of U.S. shrimp fishing; this resulted in a cessation of this fishery at the end of 1979.

In mid-1981 American shrimp fleets, which used to operate in most of the countries around the rim of the Caribbean and down the South American coast to Brazil, were active only in Guyana (ninety vessels), Cayenne (forty-three vessels), Suriname (six vessels), and Colombia (four or five vessels). Future operations in any of the Caribbean countries will depend on the extent to which the national fishermen can catch the available stocks and on bilateral licensing and other arrangements that may be made. It seems likely that the overall amount of shrimp fishing in the Caribbean will not increase significantly.

Probably the oldest U.S. fishery in the Caribbean is that for snappers. Before the turn of the century American vessels from Pensacola were making regular trips to the Campeche Banks for red snapper and for lesser amounts of other snappers and groupers. Later other Gulf cities supported snapper fleets, and this fishery continued for decades. With the extension of Mexican jurisdiction over fisheries, the conditions under which this fishery could operate changed. In 1976 the United States and Mexico agreed that the U.S. snapper-grouper vessels could fish within Mexican waters under specified licensing and other conditions. Then, on 29 December 1980, Mexico announced that this agreement would end a year later. There is a possibility that further talks will result in a renewal of some reciprocal fishing between Mexican and American vessels, but in the meantime this long-time snapper fishery is scheduled to terminate. [This fishery was terminated in December 1981.—Ed.]

Snapper fleets moved into the Caribbean after production declined from the Campeche Banks. The vessels began to fish in deep waters off Honduras and Nicaragua and off island reef areas claimed by both the United States and Colombia. A few U.S. snapper vessels (about sixteen to twenty) still operate in other parts of the Caribbean, on offshore banks from Belize to Panama. One U.S. fisherman has a license from Venezuela to fish off Aves Island.

A small amount of spiny lobster fishing has taken place by U.S. fishermen in the Caribbean. In the 1940s a U.S. vessel supplied fishermen in Belize (then called British Honduras) with gear and bought their catch for transport to Florida. This same kind of operation was carried out in other Caribbean countries. Florida lobster fishermen operated in Bahamian waters over many years, but this fishery ended following the failure in 1975 of two prolonged negotiating sessions to reach agreement on licensing and other provisions. U.S. interests have also operated lobster fisheries in Honduras and Nicaragua, although postrevolutionary developments in the latter have rendered the operations untenable.

U.S. fishermen want continued access to waters of the Caribbean. It is clear that some fishing will continue, under bilateral or joint-venture arrangements, but there seems little doubt that the heyday of this activity is past. Many Caribbean countries, led by Mexico, are working hard to increase their capacity to catch the full amount of fish available, and as this ability increases, along with higher local demands for fish, foreign fishermen will find decreasing opportunities to operate. And when they do, they will face the necessity of paying fees and adhering to a variety of regulations.

## Puerto Rico and the Virgin Islands

The United States has a special interest in the fisheries of Puerto Rico and the Virgin Islands, a U.S.-associated commonwealth and territory, respectively. Fishery production there is not large, in common with other islands of the region. In 1980 the catch in Puerto Rico was 3,276 tons and in 1979 in the American Virgin Islands 682 tons. The most valuable fishery is for spiny lobsters; in 1978 the catch in the two territories was 275 tons, valued at $1.4 million. Other species caught include king mackerel, silk and blackfin snappers, hogfish, and a very large number of small reef and bottom species caught mostly in traps. Puerto Rican and Virgin Island fisheries are handicapped by the unpredictable occurrence of ciguatera, a neurotoxin that accumulates in the flesh of some fish which can cause sickness in humans eating the affected fish.

Consumption of fish in these islands is relatively high—about seventeen pounds per capita per year, one and a half times the per capita consumption of mainland Americans. Local production falls far short of satisfying this market, and as much as three-quarters of the fish consumed is imported.

An important segment of the Puerto Rican fisheries is the tuna-processing industry, started in 1953 when a cannery was built in Ponce under the stimulation of tax concessions offered by the Government of the Commonwealth. Later three canneries were built in Mayaguez and one more in Ponce. These plants process fish from U.S.- and foreign-owned tuna vessels operating in both the eastern Pacific Ocean and the eastern Atlantic. The grounds off northern South American countries are 1,000 miles closer to Puerto Rico's than to California's ports. This industry, by far the island's largest food-processing activity, is important to its economy.

## Aquaculture

U.S. fishery interests in the Caribbean include participation in aquaculture enterprises. The culture of some species, particularly those that require warm climates, is handicapped in the continental U.S. environments, even those in the most southerly parts of the country. Of special interest are the peneid shrimps, which will grow in South Florida and along the coast of the Gulf of Mexico, but conditions there are not ideal for rapid growth or the production of more than one crop a year. Some Caribbean countries offer good climatic conditions for shrimp culture and, in some cases, offer other advantages, including access to suitable land and the availability of inexpensive labor. As a consequence the U.S. industry has moved to several Caribbean and Gulf countries to raise shrimp, among them Honduras, Panama, Costa Rica, Mexico, and Colombia. Another species which has attracted attention as a potential cultured animal is the so-called freshwater shrimp, *Macrobrachium*. Again, conditions in the tropics may be better for their growth, and operations have been set up in Costa Rica, Honduras, and Puerto Rico.

The United States has had a good deal of interest in recent years in the culture of conch. This shellfish has been a staple food of the people of a number of Caribbean countries, but with the rise in population and the pressure put on the resource by the growing tourist industry, the conch in many countries has been depleted. Efforts have been made by several research groups to develop systems for the large-scale production of conch, and U.S. scientists have been significantly involved in this. Recently a major research and development effort was launched in Puerto Rico to extend this work, and it is hoped that it will lead to a viable commercial system. [An intensive conch culture project has been conducted by the University of Miami in the Bahamas since early 1980, and a conch hatchery was opened in 1981 on Bonaire, the Netherlands Antilles. See also below, page 112.—Ed.]

## The Caribbean as a market for U.S. fishery products

The Caribbean has never been an important market for U.S. fishery products. This is partly because the United States is a small exporter of fish worldwide, exports amounting only to 12 percent of imports. Further, the kind of U.S. products available have not been those in demand in the Caribbean in general, and prices have usually been too high.

The United States is attempting to increase its fishery exports around the world, and the Caribbean is among the regions where expansion is sought. Overall, however, only a small increase of export trade in fishery products can be expected in this area.

With a few exceptions (some of the large continental countries), the nations of the Caribbean produce few cattle; they therefore depend on fish to supply a high proportion of the animal protein consumed. Caribbean people typically use 15-20 kg. of fish per capita compared to a world average of 12 kg.; in some countries of the Caribbean the amount is more than twice the world average.

Of the fish consumed in the Caribbean a high proportion is imported: in the Lesser Antilles nearly half, in the Greater Antilles about three-quarters, in some mainland countries (not including Mexico) about half. These large imports impose a heavy drain on foreign exchange.

Because of the hot climate of the Caribbean nations, the general absence of facilities for handling frozen fish, and the necessity to buy cheap fish, most that is imported has been dried, salted, or smoked—as much as 90 percent in some nations, and over half in most. Much of the remainder of the imported fish is canned.

The Caribbean countries would like to increase their own production of fish in order to reduce reliance on external sources and the drain on scarce foreign exchange. Historically the fisheries of the region have been at an artisanal level, the vessels being mostly small and primitive. Even today canoes and small boats dominate the fisheries of many countries, although in a few there are larger and more modern vessels. In several countries (e.g., Mexico, Venezuela, Guyana) there are sizable fleets of modern shrimp trawlers, some with freezer holds. Mexico has been engaged for several years in an ambitious program of expanding and modernizing her fisheries and has significantly increased her landings. Cuba has done even more in this area, building a large distant-water fleet with the help of the Soviet Union.

But these are exceptions to the rule in the Caribbean. While some of the countries have gradually improved their fleets and their production, in many cases the industry is still small and relatively primitive. There are estimated to be between 250,000 and 300,000 artisanal fishermen in the region and only about 25,000 "industrial" fishermen. Landings in 1978 in the Caribbean (as here defined) were about 500,000 metric tons, about 0.75 percent of world production.

Given the limited resources that would inhibit significantly increased catches, and assuming that the demand for fish will remain at the present level or will increase, there will be an opportunity to sell fish to the Caribbean countries. U.S. exporters should be able to share in this market to an increased degree in the future. The constraints are the kinds and forms of products wanted in Caribbean markets and the necessity to offer fish at low prices. [INFOPESCA, a marketing information and technical advisory service for the promotion of fishery products exports from Latin America, has been established by FAO and UNDP, with offices in Panama.—Ed.]

## The Caribbean as a source of seafood imports to the United States

The United States is a major market for fish, consuming 2.24 million metric tons of edible products in 1979. Of this amount, 1.5 million metric tons of edible fishery products were produced domestically that year. On the other side of the ledger this country exported only 250,000 tons of fish in 1979, valued at $1 billion, causing a trade deficit of $2.8 billion. This is of great concern since that amount represents 10 percent of the total trade deficit of the nation. Consequently, considerable efforts are being put forward to narrow the deficit in fishery trade, and a goal has been announced by the U.S. government of greatly reducing or eliminating the adverse balance. To achieve this goal will not be easy since most of the fishery products imported into this country are in great demand and are those whose domestic production cannot be increased significantly since their stocks are fully exploited. These are principally shrimp and spiny lobsters, whose high costs cause them to weigh heavily in the adverse trade balance. There is little likelihood that the demand for these products will diminish, so that changes in the amounts imported will probably be upward rather than the reverse.

In 1979 the United States imported 121,000 metric tons of shrimp worth $713 million, some 56.5 percent of the total consumed in this country. Most of this amount came from Caribbean countries, principally Mexico, Panama, Nicaragua, Colombia, Guyana, French Guiana, Guatemala, Honduras, and Venezuela.

In 1979 the United States imported about 96 percent of its supply of spiny lobsters—68,600 metric tons. About 20 percent of these imports were from Caribbean countries, among them Honduras, Mexico, The Bahamas, Nicaragua, and Belize.

In addition to shrimp and spiny lobsters, there are only relatively unimportant quantities of other fishery products imported from the Caribbean. Among them are fish fillets from Mexico and Venezuela and conch from Belize, the Bahamas, and other countries. [But see below, page 112.—Ed.] These are not likely to be major items in the near future. Nonetheless, with the high demand for shrimp and lobsters and a small but steady market for other products, the Caribbean will remain an important source of seafood for the United States.

## Oceanographic and fisheries research

The Caribbean has been the subject of intensive U.S. fishery and oceanographic research by university and government scientists for many years. It is a conveniently near part of the ocean for the study of physical, chemical, geological, and biological phenomena. Further, fishery research on the size and location of the exploitable resources of the region and on the biology of the animals has been carried out for the benefit of U.S. and foreign fishermen in the region.

U.S. government research can take credit in part for the discovery of a number of fish stocks in the Caribbean that have led to valuable fisheries. This is especially the case with shrimp. Exploratory vessels of the U.S. government, among others such as from Suriname, located grounds off Central and South America that subsequently yielded many millions of dollars worth of catch. Trials were conducted for tuna as well, and at one time there was a high expectation that the stocks would support large, industrial-scale fisheries by U.S. boats. Later it was found that the occurrence of tuna was seasonal and unpredictable; so, while some Caribbean countries catch tuna in small quantities, and the vessels of Japan and a few other foreign nations operate in these waters seasonally, U.S. tuna fleets do not fish there on a regular basis.

Other U.S. exploratory fishing efforts have revealed the presence of very large populations of herring-like fishes, which some day may support commercial fisheries. Biological studies have included life histories of the exploited animals, population dynamics, and other investigations common to such efforts. One particularly important kind of research has been to identify the origin of the recruitment for spiny lobsters. This species has been found to spend a surprisingly long time (6 to 8 months) in the pelagic larval phase. Because of the pattern and strength of the ocean currents many—perhaps most—of the spiny lobster larvae are carried considerable distances before they metamorphose and become bottom dwelling. It has therefore been suggested that the "recruitment" of lobsters to a particular fishing area is from another, more or less distant area "up" stream. There is evidence that this may not be so. But if it is true, the management implications are great, and international cooperation is obviously essential to prevent overfishing and other damage to the stocks. This unsolved biology problem is only one example of the necessity for intensive international cooperative research.

U.S. fishery interests in the Caribbean include participation in international fishery research efforts, the most important of these being the Western and Central Atlantic Fishery Commission (WECAF), organized by FAO. The area of concern for WECAF extends from the northern part of Brazil to Cape Hatteras, North Carolina. There are twenty-two member nations. The United States contributes about 20 percent of the support of WECAF. The commission sponsors and coordinates many fishery programs, including the standardization and collection of fishery statistics, the collection and analysis of biological data, and the conduct of seminars, workshops, and surveys. Many of these relate directly to the interests of the United States.

In 1968 the United States took a leading role in the formation of a coordinating program called the Cooperative Investigation of the Caribbean and Adjacent Regions (CICAR). It operated under the International Oceanographic Commission and worked with considerable success to promote cooperative international marine research in the region. Its successor, IOCARIBE, under the International Oceanographic Commission, is a coordinating body for ocean science, especially oceanography in support of fisheries. Among its projects are research on snappers and groupers, migration of lobsters, and evaluation of turtle stocks. Most of the turtle species of the area are endangered, and it is only through organizations such as IOCARIBE that the United States can generate the required international cooperation on endangered species.

There are also other fishery-related international organizations in the Caribbean through which the United States creates a valuable two-way flow of information. These include the International Commission for the Conservation of Atlantic Tunas (ICCAT), which has developed fishing regulations for yellowfin and bluefin tunas. Last, the Gulf and Caribbean Fisheries Institute of the University of Miami has brought together U.S. and Caribbean fishery scientists, industrialists, and administrators for thirty-four years.

## Conclusion

The fishery concerns of the United States in the Caribbean obviously include economic interests. For many decades U.S. fishermen have taken valuable catches from the waters of the region. The sizes of these catches are smaller than they were at one time, and they are now made under different rules, set by the coastal countries, who usually charge fees for the harvest. It seems certain that this kind of fishing will continue in the future. Second, U.S. merchants have bought seafood worth many millions of dollars from Caribbean countries, to the benefit of the economies of those nations. U.S. seafood dealers would like to increase this trade. Our merchants have sold a modest amount of seafood to the Caribbean, and they hope to increase this activity.

U.S. fishery interests in the Caribbean include the scientific. Oceanographers and fishery scientists naturally have more than ordinary curiosity about a vast and complex segment of the sea immediately adjacent to their own shores. Alone and together with various combinations of Caribbean nations, the United States has conducted many significant pure and applied fishery and oceanographic investigations. This research has helped to broaden our insight into the physical and biological phenomena of the seas in general and of the Caribbean in particular. It has also put money into the pockets of American and Caribbean fishermen and other businessmen.

And, finally, U.S. fishery interest in the Caribbean has been of the kind exhibited by neighbors and friends for the mutual welfare of a group. Former President Jimmy Carter declared that "we are a Caribbean nation just as surely as we are an Atlantic nation or a Pacific nation," and as such the United States has long reached into the area with various kinds of help and mutual activity, including a considerable amount in the fishery field. [Editor's note: Remarks by President Carter, 9 April 1980, to the Board of Trustees, Caribbean/Central American Action; *Public Papers of the Presidents of the United States: Jimmy Carter, 1980–81*, bk. 1, 624–29 (1981).] Clearly—and properly—some of this has been in support of self-interest, but a significant amount of the fishery assistance has been provided in the spirit of the principle expressed by former Secretary of State Edmund Muskie: "We must arrive at a greater appreciation of the human and physical resources of our planet. We must close the gap between the wealth that resources bring and the desperation which war and scarcity create. Doing so will require more disciplined use of resources and a better global mechanism for sharing them."

Many people, including myself, wish that the amount of neighborly help to the Caribbean in fishery matters could have been greater, yet the aggregate of such activities has been impressive: direct assistance through the Agency for International Development (AID), indirect help through United Nations agencies such as FAO and UNESCO, help from private foundations, and practical assistance in a variety of ways from U.S. universities.

Many are apprehensive about the near future of our fishery relations with Caribbean countries in the face of budget actions being taken now to overcome our nation's ominously threatening economic ills. Spending retrenchment will cancel, curtail, or postpone many valuable fishery programs supported by the federal government, and those in the Caribbean will not escape. But I am certain that these will be only temporary setbacks, dictated by harsh economic realities, and I have no doubt that the United States will maintain and eventually expand its economic, scientific, and neighborly fishery interests and activities in the Caribbean.

# Caribbean Commonwealth Fisheries: Problems and Strategies

*Julian S. Kenny*

IT WOULD be impossible, except superficially, to review the entire fisheries of the Caribbean region and the Gulf of Mexico because of their extreme diversity in this area. On the other hand, it is very tempting on the basis of some published reports (Gulland 1971, Klima 1976, Wolf & Rathjen 1974) to make the assumption that there is great potential for significant further development of fisheries throughout the area. I will suggest here that in fact, while there is scope for major development in certain select areas, the general picture for the island-states must remain bleak. Further, I will suggest that, while the overall picture is depressing, given some modification of approach to development and given some really serious subregional cooperation, there is a strong possibility that meaningful change can be effected in these states. Owing, however, to the limitations of space, I can only focus on the fisheries of comparatively few Caribbean Commonwealth countries.

The Western Central Atlantic Fisheries (WECAF) area covers approximately 16 million sq. km. of the Atlantic Ocean, the Caribbean Sea, and the Gulf of Mexico and involves directly approximately twenty-eight sovereign states with expectation of certain rights over natural resources in the adjacent seas and a still unspecified number of other states which have at some time shown some interest in the resources of the overall area. The accepted total production of fish and other marine products for the area is 1.4 million metric tons. On the surface it would appear that this not insubstantial quantity of fish could meet all of the needs of the countries in the region and possibly even permit surplus for export outside the area. On closer examination, however, it will be seen that the bulk of this production, amounting to approximately 1 million metric tons, is produced either along the Atlantic shore of the United States or in the Gulf of Mexico along the shores of both the United States and Mexico. Moreover, much of this production consists of industrial fish such as menhaden, used primarily for meal, which incidentally, may be exported to other countries in the WECAF area.

The other areas within WECAF showing some actual or potential major production are along the northeastern coast of South America in regions where there is significant upwelling or where there is major riverine discharge. There are major fisheries off Venezuela for clupeids and engraulids which are able to support canneries; in Colombia there are comparable fisheries for shrimp and demersal fishes also capable of supporting modern freezing and packaging plants. These are, however, small in comparison to the potential fishery of the Guyana Shelf between Trinidad and Venezuela in the north and Brazil in the southeast.

I am certain that other scientists will argue whether there are other areas of major potential significance. It is, of course, possible to identify areas along the Atlantic coast of Central America or the Bahamas, but the point here is that while we can accept that a resource may command varying levels of significance, depending on the size of the communities with jurisdiction over these resources, in absolute terms these particular resources remain small. This has one important significance in terms of what can realistically be done with the smaller resources. Much of the effort that has been devoted to fisheries development in the area either by the metropolitan countries or by the international organizations has been geared toward heavy capital investment and high technology. The successes have been few. The MV *Calamar,* MV *Alcyon,* and MV *Fregata,* the UNDP craft used in the exploratory fishing operations between 1965 and 1971, have been lying idle for the past six years and are up for sale. They will probably all go into the interisland trade. This approach may be acceptable and workable in the fisheries of Venezuela and Colombia and possibly those of the Guyanas, but it has no chance of success in a fishery such as might be developed in Antigua or St. Lucia. I will argue later in this paper for a different approach to fisheries development in the eastern Caribbean.

Having painted a negative picture overall for the wider Caribbean area, it is necessary to examine now the scientific basis for making the general assessment. There are two principal arguments. First, the levels of primary productivity, such as have been determined, indicate levels that are comparable with the most barren areas of the world's oceans. Levels of approximately 50–100 grams of carbon per square meter per year have been obtained in the Caribbean Sea, and there is no doubt that, overall, the mean level for the area might be less than this figure (Margalef 1968). In contrast, other parts of the

Atlantic that support major fisheries have levels of production that may be approximately 500 gC/m$^2$/yr. Indeed, if one compares the primary productivity offshore with that found in some of the mangrove lagoons in the area, where figures are as high as 1000 gC/m$^2$/yr., the inevitable conclusion must be drawn that the open seas of the Caribbean are barren.

Second, the bathymetry of the Caribbean clearly militates against any fisheries' development based on demersal stocks. The mainland countries bordering the Caribbean of course have continental shelves which support demersal stocks but, with the exception of the Bahamas and Cuba, the other Caribbean islands have simply an island shelf with deep water immediately adjacent to the land. This means that for the Caribbean island-states, the main resources to be exploited inshore will be demersal-pelagic stocks on the island shelves and offshore simply the pelagic stocks.

In addition to these two main factors there is also the general problem of the lack of any major inflow of sediments and nutrients from land masses, so that primary and secondary productivity levels inshore will not be significantly different from those obtaining offshore.

In addition to oceanographic factors that operate to limit the levels of production, there are related economic and sociological factors that have smaller effects. It is obvious that the size of any individual economy will determine the ability of that economy to create capital and to invest it in technological development. Putting it in other terms, it is extremely unlikely that an island such as Anguilla could, on its own resources, provide even the simplest processing plant obtainable from the industrialized countries. Apart from economic factors, there is the very important but frequently neglected question of cultural attitudes obtaining in underdeveloped countries. The conservatism of the artisanal fisherman in the Caribbean area is quite notable. Generally his life is, at best, a precarious hand-to-mouth existence, and he is not about to risk his limited resources in anything unproven by his culture. Taking these factors together, it is suggested that, for most of the island-states, fisheries development for the next generation must be limited to refinement of the artisanal fisheries rather than to the introduction of "modern technology."

I will now look at developments in some of the Caribbean Commonwealth countries and focus on the major problems that have arisen in each.

## Barbados

The island of Barbados is small in comparison with the other Caribbean countries, but it has an unusually high population density. It measures approximately 430 sq. km. and has a population of 250,000. Barbados presents an excellent example of what can be achieved through a combination of economic factors, sound direction, and a measure of good luck.

The island is to the windward of the other islands of the eastern Caribbean and consists of an elevated reef platform sitting on a narrow island shelf. Offshore on the shelf, there is a modest and heavily overexploited fishery of various reef species, and the bulk of the industry is geared toward exploitation of the flying fish (*Hirundichthys affinis*) and its principal predator, the dolphin (*Coryphaena hippurus*).

Up until the end of World War II, the fishery employed sailing sloops and primitive but effective hand nets for catching the flying fish. Given the continued demand for fresh fish, the fisheries officer at the time introduced a small drift gill net, which immediately increased the catch rates of the fleet. This led to further investment in the fleets in the form of mechanization of almost all of the craft, mostly through a government loan scheme and an extended range of the fishery. Although there have been other developments in the fishing industry in Barbados, notably the establishment of a trawling fleet to exploit shrimp resources in South America, the major activities of the industry remain confined to exploitation of the flying-fish stocks. Flying fish, however, appear seasonally for spawning purposes in the southeast Caribbean, and catch rates are still not high enough to provide a year-round supply of fish. One interesting development has been the importation of frozen flying-fish produce by Tobago.

One cannot be dogmatic in the absence of good data on the Barbados fishery, but the developments that have taken place during the last three decades suggest that this fishery has developed about as far as it can under existing market demand and existing availability of capital for development. To fish any farther offshore the fleet would have to be altered drastically, and it is doubtful that the resources could generate the capital to extend the range of craft from 20 km. to 200 km. Although it is suggested that further development is unlikely, the fishery serves as a good example of what might be done in the smaller communities. The high population produces the necessary market demand to stimulate production, while government inputs of capital provide the basis for establishing and developing the fleet. Not to be overlooked is the human leadership in introducing the drift gill net to replace less productive methods.

## Jamaica

In contrast to Barbados, Jamaica has approximately twenty times as much land and a population of over 2 million people. In comparison with Barbados, the resource base is probably about the same but possibly much more heavily overfished. Except on the south coast, much of the island has a narrow island shelf which supports only a small demersal fishery and coastal pelagic fisheries. In addition, some elements in the fishing community exploit similar island-shelf fisheries on the offshore keys and employ carrier boats to return catches to Jamaica.

The methods employed are, even by Caribbean standards, extremely primitive and probably reflect the general low levels of productivity in the region. Marketing is essentially a beach operation, and there is no established wholesale market or wholesale marketing system: each fishing beach is a fish market. Unlike Barbados, mechanization of the fishing fleet has been slow, and most of the craft employ outboard engines rather than inboard diesel engines. Although primitive, the fishery is innovative in some respects. For example, the Jamaican canoe, a variant of the Amerindian dugout canoe, has been replaced by a glass-reinforced plastic craft, which has more durable properties but which, curiously, is of the same narrow-beam design.

The Jamaican fishing industry is clearly still in an early developmental stage, and the main prospects for further development must lie not so much in traditional fisheries but rather in the utilization of stocks hitherto untouched. While it is perhaps surprising to observe that there are species of fish in Jamaican waters that are not currently utilized, it must be emphasized that different factors operate against the employment of new stocks of fish. The obvious ones include consumer prejudice and the special technologies needed for pelagic stocks. Shark is a delicacy in Trinidad, but it is very rarely touched in Jamaica. However, Trinidad shark, exported to Jamaica under the name of "Seaflake," sells readily in Jamaican supermarkets.

Future development of fisheries in Jamaica clearly must be based on the identification of unexploited stocks, particularly of coastal and offshore pelagics, and will require development of special technologies. Equally important will be the need for development of an adequate infrastructure.

## The Windward and Leeward islands

The Windward and Leeward islands form a chain between Trinidad in the south and Puerto Rico in the north and include former colonies of Britain, France, and The Netherlands. Although they share a common history in terms of colonization, slavery, and plantation economies, today they form a diverse group of microstates, most of which have land masses of approximately 400 sq. km. or less and populations of about 100,000 or less. Some are independent sovereign states; others remain colonies. Some are approaching independence, and one is a department of a metropolitan country.

The resource base of most of these countries is essentially similar to that of Jamaica, consisting of heavily fished demersal stocks and coastal pelagic stocks on the island shelf and still unknown quantities of offshore pelagic fishes, including migrants passing through the Caribbean Sea. Although there is some variation in detail from one island to another, the fishing industries all resemble the simple artisanal type found in Jamaica, and fishing operations are mainly a daily and casual exercise with premium fishes going to hotels and other stocks to local consumption. The methods employed are conservative, consisting of conventional hook-and-line methods, fish traps, and some beach seining.

In the absence of reliable data, it is difficult to assess the long-term prospects for further development; but, given the Barbadian development, it is not unreasonable to assume that there is some reasonable prospect for increasing production. The region to the west of the Leeward Islands, the Saba Bank, is potentially capable of supporting a significant demersal fishery such as is exploited in the Jamaican keys. One of the major problems, however, with the development of any such fishery there is the lack of the heavy capital investment necessary for procuring craft and for processing catches.

## Trinidad and Tobago

Trinidad and Tobago has the most highly developed fishing industry in the eastern Caribbean. The islands have a total area of approximately 5,100 sq. km. and a population in excess of 1 million. What is really responsible for the development of the fishery is a combination of geography and economic circumstances. Trinidad and Tobago is now reported to have the fourth highest per capita income in the Western hemisphere. Both islands lie on the continental shelf of South America and are very much influenced by the outflow of South American rivers, from the Amazon to the Orinoco, but particularly the latter. The area of shallow water amenable to exploitation by conventional methods is significantly greater than that of the other Caribbean islands; in addition, because of the effects of the Orinoco, secondary productivity is high. The UNDP trawl survey conducted in 1965–71 indicated catch rates by trawling of 500 to 1,000 kg./hr. in certain areas.

The fishing industry has a very strong artisanal basis, which has evolved over the past century from sail- and oar-propelled pirogues to fiberglass pirogues driven by outboard engines with simple chilling facilities for holding fish. The principal stocks employed in the artisanal fishery are the Spanish mackerel (*Scomberomorus brasiliensis*), various shark species, and shrimp. A wide range of fishing technology is employed, including gill nets and lampara nets. The artisanal fleet is entirely mechanized, and the industry employs a privately operated but complex system of internal transport of fish and three public wholesale fish markets. In addition to the artisanal fishery, there has developed during the last fifteen years a locally owned distant-water fleet, which was built to exploit shrimp resources off the Guyanas and Brazil, but which has since been relegated to purely local operations. The distant-water fleet is serviced by a modern shrimp- and fish-processing plant, and the capital investment has thus far amounted to $76 million. Superficially, the industry in Trinidad and Tobago appears vibrant, but this may be simply an illusion created by the heavy government support of the national fleet.

## Guyana

Guyana is included in the Caribbean because of the common historical background of its people. It is larger than the United Kingdom but has a population of less than 1 million.

Guyana has essentially the same type of resource base as Trinidad and Tobago but on a larger scale. The main stocks include the coastal pelagics and the demersal stocks, particularly the sciaenid fishes. The Guyana fishing industry has developed along lines similar to that of Trinidad, with an artisanal fishery operating in coastal waters and inland waters and, in the past few years, a distant-water fleet exploiting the continental shelf. Recently, there has been a major development of infrastructure for servicing the industry.

Of all the Caribbean countries, undoubtedly Guyana has the greatest potential for development of a fishing industry. The UNDP figures suggest that the resources of the continental shelf of Guyana, Suriname, and Cayenne can more than adequately feed the people of the Caribbean and possibly even provide all their fish-meal requirements.

## Problem areas

I have tried to focus here on the extreme diversity of type of fishery and state of development and have emphasized that there are areas, reasonably close at hand, with stocks of fish sufficiently large to meet all regional requirements.

The fact that the region, including countries such as Trinidad and Tobago, still imports fish and fish products suggests that there are serious problems affecting development.

Possibly the most significant problem is a general cultural attitude that has evolved over the past 200 years. Except in the very tiny islands, *there is no great maritime tradition, and communities have continued to use dietary habits associated with other social systems*. Possibly the economic dislocation caused by events of 1974, when the world price of oil rose sharply, might now produce the stimulus to cause the Caribbean people to look more closely to the utilization of the resources of the sea. This appears to have happened in Guyana, where there has been a major program of development of import substitutes.

Related to this problem of cultural attitudes generally, there is also the problem of the marked consumer prejudices displayed in the region. It has been mentioned that shark may be a delicacy in one country and be completely untouched in another. Flying fish is the staple of the people of Barbados but not in Grenada and St. Lucia, where it is readily available.

Related also to the historical development of the region, there is the general problem of insularity and the difficulties it presents for as simple a matter as interisland trade. It is frequently far easier to import a commodity from a metropolitan country than it is to move produce from one island-state to another. Admittedly, it is not simply a question of insularity; economic factors, including transport, have diverse effects.

So far, I have referred principally to sociological factors, but there are a number of technical problems that also adversely affect further development. Much of the trade in fish in the eastern Caribbean is on a 24-hour basis with very little effort devoted to preservation or conservation of catches, and it is not unusual for significant quantities of fish to be dumped for want of a market. The technical aspects of marketing are not insolvable, as most fish, handled well, can have enhanced shelf life as fresh or frozen fish. In most cases, however, the technical problem of marketing cannot really be solved until production levels are high enough to warrant the establishment of the necessary infrastructure.

*Perhaps one of the major problems from a scientific point of view is the general lack of knowledge of the available resources*. This problem is particularly acute in the smaller island-states, which lack entirely any sort of scientific infrastructure or any real ability to do stock assessment studies. Even in the countries with the resources, it is frequently easier to find good data on stocks in distant parts of the world than for the individual country. For example, in Trinidad and Tobago, serious biological studies have been conducted on only three species of marine fishes. *Perhaps the most important factor operating against development is the unavailability of capital and the appropriate technologies for development.* There have been numerous attempts during the last thirty years to effect development, and there has been one major resource assessment study, undertaken by the UNDP. It is significant that, certainly insofar as the eastern Caribbean is concerned, the resource assessment work was done on distant-water craft, some of the North Sea design and some of the Gulf of Mexico design, clearly with the assumption that this is what was likely to be employed in the development of the fisheries. The results overall were extremely disappointing, except for the potential shown by the Guyana continental shelf. At the same time, *it must be stressed that no serious attempt has been made to assess the inshore demersal and coastal pelagic stocks in the region or to investigate the economics of the artisanal fisheries.* It must also be emphasized that capital available from international agencies is not handed out lightly, and development banks reasonably expect to see some positive response to funding. Undoubtedly, capital will be available provided the projects are shown to be demonstrably workable.

Finally, there is one problem that needs further attention: the need for subregional action on clearly identified proposals. This is particularly obvious in the case of the Guyana shelf fisheries, which must remain underdeveloped in the absence of subregional management.

## Suggested strategies

Having listed the problems, I will now outline possible strategies for development. There are two resource base types to be considered: the island reef and coastal pelagic type and the continental shelf demersal and pelagic fisheries. The former is applicable throughout the eastern Caribbean island chain, excluding Trinidad and Tobago; the latter concerns Trinidad and Tobago and the three Guyanas.

Much of the effort employed in the Caribbean, particularly in the smaller island-states, has been, frankly, of a rather paternalistic type. What is necessary is a radically different approach. To illustrate, I need only refer to one particular event that led to the development of the shrimp-trawling industry in Trinidad about twenty-five years ago. The fisheries officer at the time built a small otter-trawl, which he employed on a fishing boat with a minimum of promotion. Initially, the response from the fishermen in the Gulf of Paria was one of jest, but when a catch of 400 pounds of shrimp was landed in the fish market at Port of Spain after approximately six hours trawling, fishermen from this fishing center descended immediately on the Fisheries Office asking for trawls. Within a fortnight, traditional land seines used for fishing shrimp were abandoned and shrimp trawls came into operation. The trawls have gradually been modified by the fishermen, but the original design remains.

This one exercise, in essence, showed the fisherman how to make more money than he had been able to do by traditional methods, which employed ten men rather than one man and a boy. *I suggest that if any organization wishes to effect meaningful development of artisanal fisheries, it must be able to show the fishermen how to make more money.* It must be emphasized that artisanal fishermen are extremely conservative people who are quite realistic in many respects. It is not unreasonable to expect a person to continue to use a tried and proven method of meeting his requirements.

Accepting that we have to show the fishermen how to make money, I think it also necessary to show him alternative resources and the possible alternative uses of existing resources. This is perhaps more complicated than simply introducing a new technology for catching fish. The reason is that general scientific knowledge of the resources of much of the Caribbean area remains extremely limited. Further development, therefore, necessitates more effective stock assessment studies, particularly of resources that are potentially usable by artisanal fisheries. I think particularly of coastal pelagic fishes such as the small jacks, clupeids, engraulids, and atherinids. Many of these island-states have stocks of these species which are only caught incidentally. Stocks of this kind, if sought particularly, might serve as a raw material for production of fish products or as raw material for supplementing feeds of one kind or another; and, given the climate, there is no reason why solar drying and a simple milling system might not produce a crude meal.

Showing fishermen how to make more money, possibly using alternative resources, will certainly require a special kind of developmental unit. In some respects, units of this kind already function in some countries, but one will have to be brought into the eastern Caribbean as the skilled manpower simply is not there. Unfortunately, every time a unit is proposed, it is very quickly filled with career bureaucrats. A good example is the recent development in WECAF meetings in Cuba, where a special case has been made for the establishment of a subunit of the commission established for the Lesser Antilles, with bureaucrats moving in and out of the area. What is really needed is people of proven practical ability to move into the area with the necessary freedom of action to pursue all aspects of the exploitation of individual resources in the area on an experimental basis.

A developmental unit of the kind proposed obviously must have the blessings not only of the international bodies and the aid-granting countries but also the countries actively involved in the region. This is probably the most difficult obstacle, as each country or each institution will be expecting its own bureaucratic interests to be furthered with scant thought for the communities particularly involved. Whether such a unit is practicable is problematical, but it is clear that none of the previous efforts have in any way been productive.

Turning to the continental-shelf fisheries to the south, there is no doubt that they constitute the major resources at the other end of the Caribbean Sea. Development of these resources requires major capital and technological input, much of which will have to come from external sources, and considerable regional accord. The alternative appears to be between the larger, diffuse, and possibly politically weak international commission involving interested members of the UN family and a smaller subregional organization involving Brazil, Cayenne, Suriname, Guyana, Venezuela, and Trinidad and Tobago. The past failures of the large-scale international commission would suggest the need to consider the other alternative.

## References

GULLAND, J. A. THE FISH RESOURCES OF THE OCEAN. Fishing News (Books) Ltd., London 1–25 (1971).

HELA, I., AND LAEVASTU, T. FISHERIES HYDROGRAPHY. Fishing News (Books) Ltd., London, 1–137 (1962).

KLIMA, E. F. A REVIEW OF THE FISHERY RESOURCES OF THE WESTERN CENTRAL ATLANTIC. WECAFC STUDIES 3, FAO, Rome, 1–77 (1976).

MARGALEF, R. *Pelagic Ecosystems in the American Mediterranean*. First CICAR Symposium, Curacao (1968).

WOLF, R. S., AND RATHJEN, W. F. *Exploratory Fishery Activities of the* UNDP/FAO *Caribbean Fishery Development Project, 1965–1971: A Summary.* MAR. FISH. REV. 36(9) 1–8 (1974).

# Comments

*Ronald W. Thompson*

I WOULD like to comment in a general way on conditions and problems as they relate to fisheries in the island nations of the Caribbean. The geography of the area is dominated by the sea, yet the surrounding ocean exercises surprisingly little beneficial influence on the outlook and lives of the inhabitants. Actually, it seems that the sea acts more as a hindrance than as a help to the people in the region. The island nations of the area are characterized by similar geographical and climatic conditions, and the islands, for the most part, are similar in appearance and in their fauna and flora.

Diversity results, however, from the wide difference of historical background, the pattern of political development, and the natural resources. Population density in some of the countries, for example Barbados, is among the highest in the world. Finding food in sufficient quantities is a problem, and it is compounded by the fact that a substantial portion of the land area is not particularly productive. Relatively large quantities of fish are consumed to help combat the resulting protein shortage, and, while some of this fish is caught in the countries, they also have to spend an important part of their limited foreign exchange to import fish.

The area has relatively low productivity, but there is another factor to consider, especially in the reef areas: although there are no great quantities of what we call "standing stock," there is a fast growth of the natural resources. Because of this growth or regeneration, we can probably exploit these resources more intensively than resources of the temperate regions. The heavily exploited fishery on the Jamaican island shelf bears testimony to this fact.

The species of fish and shellfish caught are typical of tropical seas, and species are similar all the way from the Florida Straits to Brazil. There are reef-dwelling, brackish-water, and open-water pelagic species. On the reefs a large variety of species exists, approximately 180 of which are marketed by fishermen in the region. Because these are of varying shapes and sizes, there are associated processing and marketing problems. The most important food fish inhabiting these reefs include groupers, snappers, jacks, and grunts. In the open seas, tunas, mackerels, dolphin fish, flying fish, and other pelagic species are caught, and in certain areas some of these species are important game fishes for the recreational sport of the tourist industry. Spiny lobsters, also found in some areas, are among the most valuable of the marine resources of the Caribbean. Shellfish—for example, conch, clams, and oysters—are also harvested.

A word about the gear that can be used in some of these locations: to a great extent, the use of trawls and other nets to exploit the island fishery resources of the Caribbean is precluded or severely restricted by the presence of coral reefs. In most areas the fishing techniques are restricted to the use of individually buoyed traps or fish pots or vertical lines, whether hand, mechanically, or electrically operated. Spear fishing is also an important harvesting technique, especially in shallow waters, mostly for reasons related to the low capital outlay required for this method.

Seine and gill nets are frequently used in shallow areas near reefs and on level bottoms of bays and harbors for catching jacks, groupers, and bottom-dwelling reef fish. In some areas damage to nets from contact with the coral reef or as a result of the presence of sharks limits the use of this technique. A minor portion of the reef fish in the Caribbean is taken through the use of dynamite and fish poison; in some areas toxic chemicals have caused serious damage to the coral reef. This is indeed a problem in the spiny lobster fisheries in the Bahamas.

A number of factors impede the development of fisheries in the island nations. Among them is the fact that the people living in the region do not, for the most part, have a seafaring tradition. This lack, combined with the availability of tourism-generated jobs, has made fishing an unattractive and socially inferior occupation in many of the countries of the region. In the Bahamas, for example, there are some quite successful fishermen who do not want their children to follow in their footsteps, preferring that they be doctors or lawyers.

There are also financial factors that affect the fisheries development. Funds may be available or unavailable; but even if they are available under some loan program, the fisherfolk in the small communities do not have the collateral required to obtain loans. So even the availability of funds may not solve all problems.

There is also the problem of infrastructure. The islands are dispersed, each with small population centers, so the product has to be transported to market elsewhere. Without infrastructure the catch can be sold only in the area where it is caught. The lack of holding facilities and adequate refrigerated transportation severely restricts fishery development in some countries.

As Dr. Idyll mentioned, there has been some research on resources in the area, primarily by the U.S. Fish and Wildlife Service and by UNDP. It should be pointed out that neither the U.S. exploration project nor the UNDP project really concentrated on stock assessment. Instead they did exploratory fishing, identifying what resources were there, basically the "standing stock." So, with few exceptions, it can be said that there has been little assessment of Caribbean fishery resources. One exception is the work done by the Fisheries Ecology Research Project of the University of the West Indies in Jamaica. Because of this lack of research on stock assessment, the figures quoted as maximum sustainable yields are in most instances based on stocks of fish that have been exploited heavily for some time. These figures are then applied to similar, unexploited stocks in the region to get an estimate of maximum sustainable yield. This technique is acceptable as a guideline, but to get a real idea of the resource potential of the area, there has to be additional work on unexploited and underexploited resources.

To comment briefly on recreational fishing as mentioned by Dr. Idyll: reef fishes also form an important component of the U.S. recreational fishing in the region. Vessels cruising through the Caribbean, as well as the "party boats" that have been used in recent years, catch primarily bottom-dwelling fish, and, as a result, the recreational catch of reef-dwelling species is quite significant.

Dr. Idyll mentioned the possibility of introducing bilateral licensing or other arrangements between some of the developing countries of the Caribbean and more developed countries in exploiting their stocks. I think that a number of countries in the region will probably object to this proposal because of the lack of proper monitoring and enforcement mechanisms. Because they are not entirely convinced of what is available in their waters and also because they cannot monitor what is taken, they will be reluctant to sign agreements with the developed countries. This reluctance will probably impede the expansion of the fisheries in the underdeveloped countries of the region. One thing these countries can consider is to allow the developed countries to exploit their offshore resources in areas where they exist; such activity requires large vessels, high capital investment, and a fairly high level of technology. If satisfactory agreements can be worked out between developing and developed countries to pursue this sort of fishery use, I think the island countries in the region would benefit.

In years to come, aquaculture, or fish farming, will play an increasingly important role in fishery development in the region since areas of shallow, warm, and unpolluted waters are becoming a rarity. Numerous such locations are available in the Bahamas, Turks and Caicos, Belize, and, to a lesser extent, some of the other Caribbean islands. Given the proper technology these areas can be used to farm shrimp, seaweed, and various types of marine fish. It is interesting to note the work that is being done in Puerto Rico on the conch and the similar work in the Bahamas funded by the Wallace Groves Aquaculture Foundation. This research is being carried out by the University of Miami, some of it at Whale Cay in the Bahamas and the remainder in the laboratories in Miami. By 1980 they had succeeded in rearing conch to the juvenile stage from eggs that were captured in the wild. Morton Bahamas Ltd. in Inagua, and Diamond Crystal Salt in Long Island are also embarking upon aquaculture pursuits in the Bahamas. These avenues will be pursued further in the Bahamas and elsewhere and may develop into large operations for the island communities.

Dr. Idyll indicated that, historically, the island fisheries of the region have been artisanal—mostly small and primitive. Big boats are not necessarily the solution to the area's problems; in some areas small boats are ideal for production, and what is needed is the ability to combine production from small crafts with proper storage, transportation, and adequate marketing. Small boats also help meet the employment objectives of most of the countries because many more people can be employed in the fishing industry.

Regarding U.S. exports to the Caribbean, I think the limitations that Dr. Idyll mentioned, pertaining to the present unsuitability of the U.S. products to the Caribbean market, probably will continue to result in the importation of most products from Central and South American countries, which produce a number of species and products more suited to the Caribbean region. Regarding imports into the U.S. from the region, I seriously doubt that conch is being imported from the Bahamas in significant quantities as it is illegal to export conch from the Bahamas. There might, nonetheless, be small, but certainly not large, quantities of conch being shipped out. [Processed conch meat may be exported if it is not more than 40 percent of the total product by weight. The lip of the conch shell may be exported in crushed form with the appropriate licenses. — Ed.]

A major problem in most of the countries in the Caribbean is the inability to manage the fishery resources. Financial limitations and the lack of suitably trained manpower are contributing factors. Fishery regulations in most of the islands are based largely on regulations of neighboring developing or developed countries; in some cases they are unnecessarily restrictive and impede rather than promote development. The inability to enforce regulations once they have been enacted is also a serious problem. The United Nations, as part of its assistance to the region, has conducted a number of training programs with large boats, as Professor Kenny mentioned. Candidates for the program are selected and trained; when the program has been completed, they return to what they were doing before. There needs to be a greater emphasis on the demonstration of techniques in the island communities, perhaps not far removed from the techniques presently in use, in most cases quite successfully. In this way trainees would be more inclined to follow through with practical applications after they complete the program.

In concluding, it appears natural that the Caribbean people should show a great interest in the possibility of increasing their fish production and should expect that the enormous water area promises large quantities of fish. But in considering the exploitation and the utilization of this resource, it is also necessary to consider the political, social, and economic aspects since these will determine the extent of fisheries development that will take place.

# Comments

## *James A. Storer*

UNDERLYING THE institutional aspects raised by Drs. Idyll and Kenny is the fact that they agree both about the basic limitation of the resource base and about the care that will have to be taken in the utilization of that base. Further, they agree that a large part of future growth should be based on a type of artisanal effort, the Cuban approach notwithstanding. Both talked about the required institutional mechanisms; Dr. Idyll is somewhat more optimistic than Dr. Kenny about their success or viability.

Much of the discussion about institutions focuses on the Western Central Atlantic Fisheries Commission (WECAF), one of a number of FAO commissions around the world. These commissions, catering to their own regions, provide a mechanism for countries in the region, as well as interested countries from outside, to handle problems of fisheries management and development. The commissions are associated with UNDP-FAO regional projects in each area and thus are able to have an impact on development beyond the capabilities that FAO could deliver under its regular program.

Dr. Kenny raised the question of the breadth of WECAF in terms of membership and commented that it possibly embraced too many countries as a result of the policy of open membership of any FAO commission. I am not concerned, as perhaps he is, that Zaire is a member because its membership does not impede the WECAF operation. The successful operation of WECAF is more impeded, frankly, by the failure of some of the countries in its region to participate than by open membership. It is true, however, that WECAF cannot be all things to all men nor to all parts of the subregion, and Dr. Kenny has mentioned that at the last meeting of WECAF it was proposed that a subcommittee be established to deal only with the problems in the Lesser Antilles. The United States supported this development because it feels that there are special problems in the Antilles that are not sufficiently addressed by the overall WECAF mechanism. We have also thought that in some ways a subcommittee might provide better access to funding, a most difficult problem. FAO relies on the project support it gets from UNDP to carry on these various regional efforts. In some regions FAO has also been able to attract significant amounts from bilateral donors, but the Caribbean region as a whole has not attracted as much outside bilateral support as have some of the other regions in which FAO has been active.

It must be admitted that the United States has not made substantial special contributions to fisheries. Dr. Idyll mentioned that we support 20 percent of WECAF. We do that, in effect, only because we fund 20 percent of the overall FAO budget, which supports the commissions such as WECAF. And we also make a major voluntary contribution to the larger UNDP, which funds the project activities that FAO runs in the WECAF area. We have not made special contributions earmarked for WECAF, partly because there has been a U.S. policy of one contribution to the UN agencies, not separate ones that may suit one or another department but that would upset the balance of the priorities that have been set. Oddly enough, there is an exception in the Caribbean area—IOCARIBE, an offshoot of the UNESCO International Oceanographic Commission, which provides a regional approach to oceanographic matters. The United States, through the National Oceanographic and Atmospheric Agency (NOAA), has been funding the secretariat of IOCARIBE as a direct special contribution. The United States is not precluded, of course, from carrying out assistance programs through AID that might be complementary to the activities carried out by FAO or other international organizations.

I gladly note that in 1981 AID was considering special assistance to the Lesser Antilles area in fisheries, and I hope that a specific project can be established. I share all of Dr. Kenny's concerns about the nature of the assistance we should give and about the kinds of technical experts to be provided and where they should come from. Nonetheless, these problems should not deter us from some positive actions, even though, as Dr. Idyll mentioned, we are facing some severe budget limitations. While any AID project to the Lesser Antilles would be direct bilateral assistance, we expect to cooperate fully with WECAF and its Lesser Antilles Subcommittee and we hope to do so without creating any new institutional mechanism. In that respect, I hope that this subcommittee can build on some of the useful overhead capital that is available in both WECAF and FAO and not try to duplicate for itself all of its own superstructure and staff.

In view of the general concern about the proper role of the several institutional mechanisms in this region concerned with fisheries, it might be a very useful exercise for the Gulf and Caribbean Fisheries Institute to take a hard look at the existing institutions, both governmental and nongovernmental, to examine their separate functions as well as their overall patterns. I happen to think that an organization such as the Gulf and Caribbean Fisheries Institute is particularly useful, partly because it is nongovernmental. It enjoys a good deal of professional credibility without having to bear the burdens of being a governmental organization. I believe that the institute can be more active in this area and that it could do more to bring some of the pieces together and fill some of the gaps. While it is not strictly comparable, I am reminded of another region of the world—the Indo-Pacific—where a relatively new nongovernmental but international organization has been remarkably successful in the space of a few years. That organization is the International Center for Living Aquatic Resource Management (ICLARM), which has been largely funded by the Rockefeller Foundation but now is also receiving significant contributions from USAID. It is also beginning to get support from Australia, the Federal Republic of Germany, and The Netherlands. Though getting government support, it is a nongovernmental organization with a small but an extremely competent staff able to provide a quick response in that region to requests for research, consultants, experts, and training. It is not a "bricks-and-mortar" organization so it must work very closely with the FAO, other regional organizations, research institutes, and governmental offices. In the Caribbean there isn't that same institutional mechanism working; and, while the Caribbean is a unique region and while there are a lot of different institutions and commissions operating, none is achieving its full potential, either in its own sphere of activity or in any coordinated overall action that can make the most of the Caribbean's fishery resources.

# Concluding Remarks

## *Farrokh Jhabvala*

THE STATES of the world are currently engaged in the fourth attempt in five decades to codify the Law of the Sea. No other area of international law comes easily to mind that may be said to have been the focus of so much attention. The latest effort, which officially began in 1974 and has continued through the intervening years, is by far the most ambitious of all the efforts at codification, including as it does about 160 negotiating parties and interests that have been expressed in a text of 320 articles and 8 annexes spanning some 180 pages of closely printed material. This unprecedented international effort has recently suffered a setback from the U.S.-induced pause in final negotiations when, indeed, it appeared even to jaded observers that it was on the verge of successful conclusion. Notwithstanding this setback, the Law of the Sea Treaty may yet become part of international law. [The treaty was signed in Jamaica on 10 December 1982.—Ed.]

The previous "successful" effort took place in Geneva in 1958, when four separate treaties were concluded. These treaties, however, failed to receive the unambiguous support of states as expressed through ratifications and accessions. The UN secretary-general's compilation of the status of multilateral treaties reports that as of 31 December 1979, only 56 states had accepted the High Seas Convention, 45 the Convention on the Territorial Sea and Contiguous Zone, 53 the Continental Shelf Convention, and 35 that on Fisheries and the Conservation of Living Resources. Of the several colonies, overseas departments, and other quasi-independent entities in the Caribbean region on whose behalf these treaties were signed by European colonial powers, only two, Jamaica and Trinidad and Tobago, deposited notifications of succession to these treaties upon attaining self-determination. Of about 25 states that may be considered Caribbean, only 11 have clearly accepted the High Seas Convention, 9 the Territorial Sea–Contiguous Zone Convention, 13 the Continental Shelf Convention, and 11 the one on Fisheries and Conservation. Included in these numbers are four states—the U.S., the U.K., France, and The Netherlands—which have accepted these treaties more for the protection of their global interests than for regional Caribbean reasons. Thus, at least by the yardstick of the number of ratifications, accessions, and successions, the 1958 Geneva conventions clearly received only indifferent support from states in general and from Caribbean states in particular.

Apart from the lack of clear support, the 1958 treaties were also relatively short lived in a practical or political sense, although they continue, undoubtedly, to be treaties in force for their respective parties. The four conventions came into force at various times between September 1962 and March 1966. By the late sixties they were already being called into question, and by the early seventies the preparatory work to supersede them was well under way. They enjoyed a very brief span of effectiveness.

Some of the reasons for this turn of events may be found in the world of 1958. The membership of the United Nations stood at 82 in that year, and, according to the yearbook of the UN, 86 states participated in the Geneva Law of the Sea Conference of that year. Almost all of Africa, along with parts of Asia, the Caribbean, and the Pacific, had yet to attain self-determination. This was to prove to be an important political factor in the early obsolescence of the 1958 treaties. The great question of socioeconomic development was naively viewed at the time as the simple implementation of existing, largely Western, models of economic growth; and, while scarcities of energy and important hard minerals had been predicted from time to time, their true impact was even then more than a decade in the future. The radical change in the political complexion of the world that has occurred during the sixties and seventies and the palpable demonstration of the failure of the development models of the fifties were reasons of the first order in the call for a new Law of the Sea.

Other reasons for the early obsolescence of the Geneva treaties may be found in phenomena that had been set in motion prior to 1958. Humanity's uses of the oceans, for navigation, trade, security, and fishing, had remained fairly constant until the latter half of the nineteenth century, when the laying of submarine cables added the new function of transoceanic communication to the historic uses of the seas. And, as the pace of technological change quickened through the late nineteenth and early twentieth centuries, newer uses of the oceans came to be established: for submarine navigation, for overflights, and for the recovery of offshore resources. The 1942 Anglo-Venezuelan treaty on the submarine areas of the Gulf of Paria and the 1945 Truman Declaration on the continental shelf may be mentioned in connection with the recovery of offshore resources. Kaldone Nweihed has drawn attention to the fact that both the treaty and the declaration were responses to developments in the Caribbean region, broadly defined. The 1958 treaties were ill equipped to deal with, and to regulate, the exploitation of the vast resource potentials of the oceans in a manner that would distribute benefits fairly to all states. The approach, if one is to generalize, was essentially laissez-faire. And, recoiling from this state of affairs, developing states attempted to set up not only an international regime to regulate the recovery of resources and their wider distribution but also to establish, as far as developing coastal states were concerned, extensive zones of control to preserve, where possible, resources for their future needs.

Thus, among the clearest departures from the 1958 treaties has been the establishment of the relatively new concept of the exclusive economic zone, a 200-mile-wide zone where possible, in which the coastal state has sovereign rights for exploring, managing, and using the resources of the water, the seabed, and the subsoil included within the zone. Many writers have pointed out that the notion of the exclusive economic zone was first enunciated as the "patrimonial sea" at the 1972 specialized conference of the Caribbean countries on problems of the sea. The majority of states in the Caribbean region have by now declared 200-mile zones of one sort or another. [As of 1 March 1982, the Office of the Geographer, U. S. Department of State, had listed two states that claimed 200-mile territorial seas, 14 that claimed 200-mile economic zones, and one that claimed the more limited 200-mile fishing zone—a total of 17 states in the Caribbean region. Worldwide, 56 states had declared 200-mile exclusive economic zones by March 1982, another 23 claimed 200-mile fishing zones, and 14 claimed 200-mile territorial seas. It is worth noting that, of the 56 states, including Caribbean states, that have declared 200-mile economic zones, only six—France, Iceland, New Zealand, Norway, Portugal, and Spain—are not members of the Group of 77. Eight of the 23 others that claim 200-mile fishing zones and all 15 that claim 200-mile territorial seas are members of that group.—Ed.]

The development of the "common heritage" principle by the Third World to govern activities on the seabed beyond the limits of national jurisdiction was also motivated by the desire to ensure the equitable division of resources for future developmental purposes. Sharing these interests generally with other developing states, Caribbean states—not including the United States—have supported these concepts, although in some cases the support has been with qualifications, as Professor Vaughan Lewis pointed out. And, as Lennox Ballah showed, the potential benefits for developing states from a new Law of the Sea may have been overstated.

A quick glance at a map of the Caribbean that depicts 200-mile zones reveals that the entire Caribbean Sea and all but a tiny sliver of the Gulf of Mexico fall within such zones. The delimitation of the boundaries between the different national zones thus becomes a pressing matter in the Caribbean, for the lack of definition of the contours of these zones reduces the ability of states to protect those very interests that prompted the 200-mile declarations in the first place. As Kaldone Nweihed described, several delimitation agreements have already been concluded; but, according to his calculations, more than 90 delimitations remain to be undertaken. Whether these delimitations will in fact be undertaken is not clear at this stage.

It is not even clear that all states in the Caribbean will declare 200-mile zones. Lewis and Ballah have rightly pointed out that all states do not stand to gain through general declarations of 200-mile zones. States that have historically or traditionally depended on access to fishing grounds off the coasts of other states stand to suffer from the extension of exclusive or preferential coastal state jurisdictions over fishery resources. The unilateral extension of Iceland's reserved fishing zone, for instance, and the attempted exclusion of British fishermen who had traditionally fished in these waters led to the so-called Cod War between the two countries. In the Caribbean the extension of coastal-state jurisdiction to 200 miles will affect adversely the fishing interests of other Caribbean states, such as Jamaica and Trinidad. These states have held back from declaring their own 200-mile zones because such declarations may preempt or preclude access to the exclusive economic or fishing zones of other states to which they have traditionally had access.

The physical setting of the insular Caribbean states also works to their disadvantage; they stand to gain relatively small portions of ocean space through 200-mile declarations. The need to compensate states for such geographical disadvantage has been recognized in the text of the draft Law of the Sea Treaty, although with qualifications. Article 70 of the ninth session's draft describes "States with special geographical characteristics" as including "States bordering enclosed or semi-enclosed seas, whose geographical situation makes them dependent upon the exploitation of the living resources of the exclusive economic zones of other States in the subregion or region for adequate supplies of fish for the nutritional purposes of their populations or parts thereof. . . ." Such states, which clearly include the island Caribbean states, "shall have the right to participate, on an equitable basis, in the exploitation of an appropriate part of the surplus of the living resources of the exclusive economic zones of coastal States of the same subregion or region. . . ." The realization of such a right depends, *inter alia*, upon the existence of a surplus, upon nutritional needs, and upon the attainment of a mutually satisfactory agreement between the two states concerned. The examples mentioned by Lewis and Kenny—Jamaica with Colombia, Barbados with Brazil, and Trinidad with Guyana and Brazil—illustrate the point.

The conclusion and the coming into force of a global Law of the Sea Treaty that recognizes 200-mile economic zones will perhaps put some pressure on the states holding out at present from declaring their own exclusive economic zones. On the other hand, the discovery of offshore resources of oil and natural gas could change this situation rapidly. And if delimitations are perceived as being necessary, both equity and equidistance will have their place, as pointed out by Lewis Alexander.

Professor Kenny and Dr. Idyll have explained the scientific reasons for the relative paucity of large-scale fisheries in the Caribbean. They share the conclusion that there are no large underexploited stocks of fish in the Caribbean Sea that can support industrial-scale fisheries in the islands. Kenny's analysis of fisheries in the Caribbean Commonwealth countries points clearly to Guyana as the state with the present potential for developing a fishing industry. According to the Interamerican Development Bank's report on Economic and Social Progress in Latin America, fisheries contributed less than 4 percent of the GDP of Guyana in 1977. The 1978 report of the Interamerican Bank noted "no real growth in the fishery . . . subsector." Clearly, this situation is likely to change in the future. After some planning and preliminary studies, Guyana requested assistance from the Interamerican Bank in 1980 to build a modern fishing fleet.

While the Caribbean island states may not be as advantageously situated as Guyana in terms of potential fisheries, both Professor Kenny and Mr. Thompson suggest that, were an inventory of fish stocks to be taken, one might discover a potential for the development and modest expansion of Caribbean island fisheries. Their warnings: Stay away from heavy capital investment and high technology; concentrate upon appropriate technologies and rely upon small development units staffed by experts who will demonstrate the financial gains to be made from improvements in current techniques. Kenny also strongly recommends the creation of subregional organizations that may undertake the necessary surveys and assist with the development of the fisheries. Mr. Thompson has suggested the development of fish cooperatives where the harvesting activity would be conducted on a small scale, but the coops would provide credit and larger-scale processing, refrigeration, and marketing.

Clearly, no discussion of maritime interests in the Caribbean can be complete without a recognition of U. S. interests in the region. Vaughan Lewis has categorized these interests as both general and particular. The main general U. S. interests in the Caribbean region are broadly those that reflect its superpower status, including such strategic and security interests as free navigation, both on the surface and underwater, and free overflight. U. S. interests in the Caribbean also include the protection of a variety of economic investments in the countries of the area and the maintenance of open channels of access to its Gulf ports and to southeast Atlantic ports such as Miami and Port Everglades. Major resource interests in the sea are those of potential and actual oil and natural gas reserves in the Gulf rather than commercial fisheries, which, as Dr. Idyll described, have been contracting and are smaller than they were a few years ago. And this includes the shrimp fisheries.

General U. S. interests in the region also include the promotion and maintenance of a favorable political and legal order. It must be added that there are clear limits established both by global and regional arrangements, treaties and customs, within which alone such promotional activity may be conducted. Experience indicates that the general U. S. attitude toward the Caribbean may at best be characterized as one of neglect punctuated by brief spells of nervous activity in response to perceived threats to the United States or its interests. Such a policy, if one may be forgiven for using the term loosely, has repeatedly failed, leading the United States to violate repeatedly those fundamental international standards whose violations by others it so strenuously condemns. It must be recognized that the promotion and maintenance of a favorable political and legal order can be achieved only at a price. Current U. S. policy toward the Caribbean may be described as "penny-wise but pound-foolish." It saves pennies on development and other peaceful assistance but feels compelled to spend pounds on emergency military and security assistance and intervention.

The pennies of development assistance must include U. S. support through both bilateral and multilateral channels for the development and management of Caribbean island fisheries, as Idyll has described. The caveats regarding appropriate technologies and indigenous development mentioned by Kenny will be critical here if we are to avoid the conclusion of Santayana's well-known saying: those who cannot remember the past are condemned to repeat it. U. S. assistance should also include easier access to U. S. markets for a broader range of fishery exports, including processed items, from the Caribbean states, with any adjustment that may be necessitated by U. S. trade imbalances being placed upon states better able to bear such burdens. The equitable sharing of scientific and technical knowledge may be another element of the price for the United States.

Such activity could perhaps be best undertaken through regional or subregional organizations. Indeed, the unanimous element in all the papers was the expressed need for such institutions, and Ballah has called for a new regional conference on the Caribbean. In the establishment of any such institution, however, a reasonably large mix of total resources and interests will have to be included, as Lewis and Nweihed have foreseen and Ballah has elaborated. This condition appears to be imposed by the need for institutional flexibility so that the necessary trade-offs may be struck. In his book *The Twenty-ninth Day*, Lester Brown argues that only a planetary bargain can adequately address the world's problems. Perhaps in a similar vein but at a lower level of generalization, this conference has illuminated the need for a Caribbean maritime bargain that will include all the states of the region and will assist through appropriate regional units the fulfillment of the maritime interests of the Caribbean states.

# Index